PRESERVED
Drinks

VOLUME 3

PRESERVED

Drinks

DARRA GOLDSTEIN / CORTNEY BURNS / RICHARD MARTIN

PHOTOGRAPHY BY DAVID MALOSH

Hardie Grant

NORTH AMERICA

CONTENTS

RECIPES

A Toast to Drinks

Occasions both joyous and sorrowful are marked with drinks, and the rituals surrounding them perpetuate deeply held cultural traditions.

From the earliest times, people have thirsted for more than water to drink. By 7000 BCE, the Chinese were fermenting rice, honey, and fruit into the world's oldest known alcoholic beverage. By 6000 BCE, grape wine was being made in Georgia, and barley beer in southern Babylonia. These early alcoholic drinks were considered gifts from the gods, and people developed rituals around them to honor or appease the deities who determined their fate. The gods, in turn, protected those who made these offerings. Millennia later, occasions both joyous and sorrowful are still formally marked with drinks, and the rituals surrounding them perpetuate deeply held cultural traditions. When we imbibe, whether pouring a libation or raising a toast, we share in community.

The cultural significance of drinks is underscored by the extraordinary vessels that have been created to serve them. Among the first of these were drinking horns made from the polished horns of rams or aurochs and often embellished with rims of silver. Passing a horn hand to hand, imbibers praised the gods who had bestowed the wine or beer they were sharing, a practice that eventually evolved into the toasting we're familiar with today. In medieval England, two-handled loving cups—later immortalized in a song by the Rolling Stones—were communally passed as a sign of fraternity.

Expanding trade routes brought distilled alcohol, tea, and coffee to Europe from Asia and Africa, giving rise not just to novel forms of pleasure but also to magical thinking. Fortune tellers and oracles invested coffee and tea with meaning beyond the beverage itself, divining the future by reading the tea leaves or coffee grounds left behind after the brewed liquid had been drunk. The new beverages also spurred enduring societal changes. Along the Silk Road through Central Asia, merchants stopped at chaikhanas to drink tea and share the latest news. Once coffee was introduced to Europe in the sixteenth century, coffeehouses began to appear, transforming public life as writers, artists, and political activists gathered to debate often subversive ideas. Such contemporary social institutions as the downhome American kaffeeklatsch and Sweden's fika— a near-mandatory morning coffee break—are enduring outgrowths of these coffeehouses. Coffee also infiltrated language: *fika* is an inversion of *kaffi*, a slang term for coffee. And in Turkey, the word for brown is kahverengi ("coffee-colored"), which, as coffee spread throughout the Ottoman Empire, displaced other, earlier ways of saying "brown."

Many of the world's most beloved drinks are products of fermentation: beans for coffee and hot chocolate; leaves for tea; grapes for wine; agave for mezcal; maize for chicha; and grains for beer, sake, and distilled alcohols like whiskey and vodka. In this book, which is part of a series devoted to preservation, we didn't want to neglect these fundamental beverages and the customs they express. But they're not easy to make at home. So instead of offering recipes requiring a winepress, fermentation tank, or moonshine still, we've highlighted these beverages in mini essays and in images, devoting our recipes to drinks that are more doable in a home kitchen.

These include some of our favorite nonalcoholic fermented drinks, like Finnish sima (a sparkly lemonade), Russian pear kvass, and sarsaparilla soda, a precursor to root beer. We especially like to make sodas by means of natural fermentation, letting the wild yeasts on the fruit and in the air do their job. These sodas don't have the same kind of powerful fizz that you find in commercial brands; in these subtler drinks, carbonation is secondary, allowing the flavors of the ingredients to shine. Better yet, these sodas are not laden with sugar. They are, in fact, healthy, providing goodly amounts of probiotics and prebiotics, both of which encourage healthy gut microflora.

This volume offers instructions for making some of the world's most exciting beverages. You'll taste Mexico in our mango tepache and corn tejuino, and El Salvador in the horchata that starts with morro seeds from the calabash tree. We turned to India for our sweet and salty lassis, and to Turkey for şalgam, a bracing drink fermented from purple carrots and bulgur. Sweden gives us julmust, a gingerbread-flavored drink based on malted barley and rye, and Denmark offers white gløgg, a mulled wine. Some of these drinks are admittedly old-fashioned, like our wintry aged eggnog and summery switchel with fresh berries. Others are more newfangled, like strawberry-anise whey soda and charred rhubarb and lilac cordial. Not all of them are intended for long keeping, but others, such as amaro, pompelmocello (a grapefruit liqueur), and fire cider, will keep virtually forever.

Cherry Soda

Soda can easily be returned to its roots as a wild-fermented drink by using a natural starter called a "bug." All you have to do is let the bug ferment and then add it to any clear fruit juice. Ginger bug gets its name from the good microbes—the bugs—that are plentiful on gingerroot. When this wild yeast comes into contact with water and a little sugar, lactic acid fermentation begins. Ginger drinks have long been popular in the plant's native India, which is also where the technology of processing sugarcane first developed. Colonial powers introduced ginger and sugarcane to Europe and later to the Americas. Both crops thrived in the Caribbean, where the forced labor of enslaved people brought the plantation owners huge profits. Not surprisingly, these colonizers also developed a liking for ginger drinks, especially ginger beer. Like kombucha, ginger beer was made with a SCOBY, a mixed culture of bacteria and yeast. By the eighteenth century, ginger drinks had become enormously popular in both Britain and the American colonies; using a bug instead of a SCOBY made the fermentation process that much easier.

1 quart / 1 L sour cherry juice or other
    unsweetened fruit juice
½ cup / 120 ml strained Ginger-Turmeric Bug
    (page 8)

In a 6-cup / 1.5 L nonreactive container, combine the cherry juice and the bug. Cover the container with cheesecloth and secure with a rubber band. Let stand out of direct sunlight at room temperature, ideally between 65°F and 72°F / 18°C and 22°C, until the mixture is slightly foamy and releases bubbles when stirred, 3 to 4 days. If mold forms on the surface, carefully skim it off.

Transfer the liquid to one or more flip-top bottles or canning jars with tight-fitting lids, leaving at least 1 inch / 2.5 cm of head space to allow the carbon dioxide to expand. Let stand at room temperature until small bubbles form, about 24 hours. Refrigerate for up to 1 month. Serve cold straight out of the bottle or over ice.

Ginger-Turmeric Bug

This natural starter can be used to carbonate all sorts of beverages, including Cherry Soda (page 7) and Sweet Potato Fly (page 79). If you can't find fresh turmeric, it's fine to use all gingerroot, though turmeric offers a lovely counterpoint to ginger's bite. Like a sourdough mother, the bug can be put to sleep in the refrigerator for extended periods of time, as long as you keep it alive with weekly additions of grated ginger or turmeric and sugar.

2 cups / 475 ml filtered water

¼ cup / 24 g finely grated unpeeled fresh gingerroot

¼ cup / 24 g finely grated unpeeled fresh turmeric

8 tablespoons / 94 g sugar

In a 1-quart / 1 L jar, combine the water, 1 tablespoon each of the ginger and turmeric, and 2 tablespoons of the sugar. Cover the mouth of the jar with cheesecloth, secure it with a rubber band, and let the mixture stand overnight at room temperature and out of direct sunlight. The next day, add another 1½ teaspoons each of ginger and turmeric and 1 tablespoon of sugar to feed the starter. Continue feeding the starter for 5 more days, at which point it should have begun to bubble and foam. The starter is now ready to use.

If you are not using the starter right away, cover and refrigerate it. If you feed it once a week with an additional 1½ teaspoons each of ginger and turmeric and 1 tablespoon of sugar, it will last more or less indefinitely. When you are ready to make soda, bring the starter to room temperature and feed it daily with 1½ teaspoons each of ginger and turmeric and 1 tablespoon of sugar until it is bubbly again, about 3 days.

White Gløgg

In Europe, hot spiced drinks evolved from the Romans, who appreciated both the sooth-ing powers of hot wines in winter and the medicinal effects of the spices. Medieval British cooks similarly believed in the health benefits of mulled wine and named their version "hippocras," after the ancient Greek physician. Older styles of hot drinks fell out of favor in the nineteenth century as people came to prefer lighter beverages, but these drinks have remained embedded in Christmas traditions, especially in Scandi-navia, where the aroma of simmering spices in mulled wine perfumes the air.

The irons used to make mulled wine were also known as loggerheads. They had a long handle with a bulbous end that was inserted into the embers on a hearth until red hot. Then the iron was quickly placed in the drink, causing much hissing and steaming. These mulling irons had an alternate use on wooden ships, where they were employed to melt pitch for sealing the decks. They also proved to be handy weapons. Sailors often reached for their heating irons when they were "at loggerheads"—in strong dis-agreement. Thankfully, the use of these tools was more convivial in the kitchen.

Mulled wine is usually made with red wine, but we're partial to a lighter style prepared with white wine. And you don't have to wait for cold weather to enjoy it. Try this gløgg chilled as an aperitif, or mix it with sparkling water for a summery spritzer.

---

1 (8-ounce/225 g) parsnip, unpeeled

1 tablespoon honey

1 tablespoon orange juice

2 (750 ml) bottles fruity, dry, unoaked white wine, such as dry riesling or sauvignon blanc

750 ml apple cider (about 3 cups)

2 large, ripe pears, cut in ½-inch/1.25 cm slices

1 small lemon, thinly sliced

1 (2-inch/5 cm) knob of ginger, peeled and sliced very thin or minced

1 cinnamon stick

8 cardamom pods, cracked open

6 cloves

16 juniper berries

1 tablespoon white peppercorns

2 teaspoons coriander seed, toasted

1 tablespoon aniseed, toasted

2 whole star anise

1 bay leaf

2 teaspoons almond extract

¼ cup/85 g honey

1½ cups/360 ml elderflower liqueur

1 cup/240 ml white rum

Preheat the oven to 375°F/190°C. Slice the parsnip in half lengthwise, then place the flat sides down on a cutting board and slice into ¼-inch/.6 cm half-moons. Place the parsnip in a bowl and toss with the honey and orange juice. Transfer to a baking sheet and roast on the middle shelf of the oven for 20 minutes, stirring once halfway through, until slightly golden on the edges. Set aside.

In a heavy pot or Dutch oven, combine the wine, roasted parsnips, cider, pears, lemon, ginger, and spices and bring to a simmer over medium heat. Cover the pot and simmer on low for 30 minutes, then turn off the heat and leave the mixture to infuse for 4 hours.

Stir in the almond extract and honey and let the mixture sit for 15 minutes more, then strain into a clean pot through a fine-mesh strainer. Stir in the elderflower liqueur and the rum. To serve immediately, rewarm the gløgg over low heat, or bottle it and refrigerate until ready to use. It will keep for 3 months.

The Kula

Though Georgians commonly serve wine in glasses, they often bring out old-fashioned drinking vessels for a traditional feast—the supra—to highlight the reverence they feel for wine. These vessels include animal-shaped jugs with a drinking spout that forms the animal's head, suggesting connections with the pre-Christian pagan world. Another vessel is a shallow, bowl-like goblet made by smoking red clay in the kiln to turn it a distinctive shade of black. Also a favorite is a polished ram's horn, which can't be safely set down until each drinker has emptied the contents. Gourd-shaped kulas demand similar treatment. Made of wood, they're ornately carved and decorated with metal filigree. The kula has only one small opening, at the end of a long handle that also serves as the drinking spout. Georgians raise elaborate toasts to praise the fruit of the vine. Since wine is so intrinsic to Georgian heritage and identity, it's considered an insult if guests, particularly men, decline to drink each round of wine.

Deep in the Caucasus Mountains lies the small country of Georgia, home to *Vitis vinifera*, the original wine grape. Winemaking in Georgia reaches back an astonishing 8,000 years, and the traditional methods for making wine and rituals for drinking it are still practiced today.

At the heart of the Georgian winemaking tradition is the qvevri, a clay fermentation vessel that is buried in the ground, where the earth's cool, steady temperature allows desirable yeasts to flourish. Georgian wines, even white ones, are traditionally fermented with the grape skins, stems, and seeds. The "orange" wine that's so trendy today has been made in Georgia for thousands of years.

A Quintet of Cordials

The Latin root cor *lies at the heart of the drinks known as cordials, and appropriately so, as its meaning is literally "heart."* Cordial *is often used as a synonym for sweet liqueur with a low alcohol content, but here we call on an older meaning of the word, which refers to a drink with properties beneficial to the heart. Such cordials were concocted by apothecaries; beyond their medicinal use, many were considered aphrodisiac. We offer five versions of cordials below, three of them nonalcoholic, so you can truly drink to your heart's content.*

To serve all of these cordials, mix them with water, soda water, or sparkling water, in a ratio of 1 part cordial to 3 parts water. If you want a bit more acidity, add a splash of citrus juice. The cordials are also lovely mixed into cocktails for an invigorating drink.

PRESERVED LEMON OLEO
MAKES ABOUT 1 CUP / 240 ML

"Oleo" is shorthand for "oleosaccharum," in which the oil from citrus peels (the oleo) is mixed with sugar (the saccharum). This intensely flavored "sugar oil" was once considered a necessary ingredient for punch. In the past, lemons were energetically rubbed against hard cones of sugar until all of the oily peel had been grated off. These days, you can simply peel the fruit with a Y-shaped peeler.

Instead of discarding the solids after you've strained them out of the liquid, try adding them to a pint of vodka and leaving the mixture to infuse for a couple of weeks. Or chop them and add to a bowl of yogurt, or to fruitcake batter, or mix them with ricotta for a lemony tang.

8 unwaxed organic lemons
1 preserved lemon
1 heaping cup / 220 g superfine (caster) sugar

With a peeler, remove the outer rind from the lemons, being careful to avoid the bitter white pith. Cut the preserved lemon in half, remove the seeds, and chop the lemon finely. Place all of the zest and the chopped preserved lemon in a medium bowl and toss it with the sugar. With a muddler, pound the mixture a bit to extract the oils, then cover the bowl and let the sugar sit for at least 8 hours and up to 1 day, muddling and mixing every few hours to ensure that all of the sugar dissolves and as much oil as possible is extracted from the zest.

The next day, strain the citrus liquid through a fine-mesh strainer, pushing hard on the solids to release as much liquid as possible. Pour the cordial into a small bottle and refrigerate until ready to use. The mixture will keep, refrigerated, for 1 month.

PASSION FRUIT AND MINT CORDIAL
MAKES ABOUT 2 CUPS / 480 ML

This bright, refreshing summertime cordial is a favorite of ours. If you're lucky enough to have access to fresh passion fruits, cut them in half and scoop out the flesh, seeds and all. Otherwise, unsweetened passion fruit purée makes a fine substitute. CONTINUED ▶

1 cup/240 ml fresh passion fruit pulp from
    about 12 passion fruits (or substitute
    ¾ cup/180 ml unsweetened passion
    fruit purée)
2 tablespoons tightly packed fresh mint leaves
½ vanilla bean
1 cup/200 g superfine (caster) sugar
1 cup/240 ml freshly squeezed lemon juice

Spoon the passion fruit pulp into a mixing bowl.
Add the mint.

Slice the vanilla bean in half vertically and
scrape the seeds into a small saucepan. Drop
in the bean and stir in the sugar and lemon
juice. Warm the mixture over medium heat,
stirring constantly, until the sugar dissolves;
do not let it boil. Pour the sugar mixture into
the bowl with the passion fruit pulp and mint.
Stir to combine and leave to macerate until
cool, about 45 minutes.

Remove the vanilla bean and mint leaves; if
you want to remove the passion fruit seeds,
pour the mixture through a fine-mesh strainer.
Transfer the cordial to a sealable bottle and
refrigerate until ready to use. The mixture will
keep in the refrigerator for at least 3 weeks; for
longer storage, gently simmer the prepared
cordial for a few minutes over low heat before
pouring it into a bottle.

CHARRED RHUBARB AND LILAC CORDIAL

MAKES ABOUT 3 CUPS / 720 ML

*When spring is in the air, we like to
make a syrup that combines two of our
favorite harbingers of the season—bright
red stalks of rhubarb and pale-lavender
lilac blossoms. To add a slightly smoky
taste, we lightly char half the rhubarb
before simmering it with the blossoms and
sugar. Add this pretty pink syrup to sparkling water or freshly squeezed lemonade*

*for a refreshing cordial, or turn it into a
cocktail by mixing it with muddled raw
rhubarb and tequila (recipe follows). For a
memory of springtime even after the last
leaves have fallen from the trees, freeze the
syrup in ice cube trays.*

1 pound/454 g red rhubarb
1¼ cups/250 g sugar
2½ cups/590 ml water
½ cup/120 ml freshly squeezed lemon juice
⅛ teaspoon salt
½ cup tightly packed/16 g freshly picked lilac
    flowers or 2 tablespoons dried lavender
Sparkling water

Divide the rhubarb in half, setting aside
½ pound/225 g for simmering.

To char the remaining rhubarb, cut it into
4- to 5-inch/10 to 12 cm planks. Set a metal
cooling rack directly over a gas burner with a
medium-high flame and heat it until quite hot.
Alternatively, prepare a grill with medium heat,
or set an oven rack 3 to 4 inches/7.5 to 10 cm
below the broiler. Char the rhubarb, turning
it frequently so that it doesn't burn, until the
stalks are browned in places but still firm and
crisp. Cool to room temperature.

Cut both the raw and charred rhubarb into
½-inch/1.25 cm pieces and place in a saucepan with the sugar, water, lemon juice, salt,
and flowers. Simmer on low heat for 15 to
20 minutes, stirring and smashing the rhubarb
gently as it cooks until it has broken down and
released its juices.

Allow the mixture to cool for 15 minutes, then
strain through a fine-mesh strainer lined with
cheesecloth. Wring out the cheesecloth to
extract as much juice as possible. You can save
the rhubarb pulp for a yogurt bowl or purée it
into a smoothie. CONTINUED ▶

Pour the syrup into a clean 3-cup/750 ml glass bottle or jar. It will keep in the refrigerator for 1 month and in the freezer for at least 6 months (pour the syrup into ice cube trays for freezing so that small amounts can quickly be thawed).

To make the cordial, for each 1 cup/240 ml sparkling water, add 3 tablespoons/45 ml syrup, or more to taste.

TEQUILA SOUR
MAKES 2 COCKTAILS

1 small stalk of rhubarb, cut into ¼-inch/
    .6 cm slices
½ teaspoon sucanat or granulated or light
    brown sugar
2 ounces/60 ml blanco tequila
2 ounces/60 ml reposado tequila
1½ tablespoons freshly squeezed lemon juice
1½ tablespoons freshly squeezed lime juice
5 tablespoons/75 ml Charred Rhubarb and
    Lilac Cordial
3 tablespoons/45 ml Cointreau
Ice

Place the rhubarb and sucanat in a cocktail shaker and muddle hard to break the rhubarb down. Add the tequilas, lemon and lime juices, cordial, and Cointreau, then add a generous handful of ice. Cover and shake vigorously for 30 seconds. Strain the mixture into chilled martini glasses and serve immediately.

PRESERVED PLUM CORDIAL
MAKES ABOUT 3 CUPS / 750 ML

This recipe uses plums three ways—fresh, fermented, and salted—to create a fruity cordial that can also be mixed into smoothies or spooned over yogurt or ice cream.

LACTO-FERMENTED PLUM PULP
7 ounces/200 g pitted plums
½ teaspoon/2 g kosher salt

PLUM CORDIAL
1¼ pounds/560 g pitted plums
¾ cup/200 g Lacto-Fermented Plum Pulp
2 umeboshi (Japanese pickled plums), pitted
Scant ¾ cup/135 g sugar
3 tablespoons/45 ml freshly squeezed
    lemon juice

Gently pulse the plums and salt together in a blender. Transfer the pulp to a glass jar and cover tightly with a lid. Leave the plums to ferment at room temperature (68° to 72°F / 20° to 22°C) for 3 days, stirring once a day.

Place the fresh plums, plum pulp, umeboshi, sugar, and lemon juice in a blender and mix on high speed for 1 minute to make a smooth purée. Strain the mixture through a fine-mesh sieve. Transfer it through a funnel into a 3-cup/750 ml bottle and seal well. The cordial will keep, refrigerated, for 3 months or more.

SUMMER FRUIT AND LICHEN CORDIAL
MAKES ABOUT 1 QUART / 1 L

Thanks to its use of summer berries and reindeer lichen (also known as reindeer moss, Cladonia rangiferina), this gorgeous purple cordial has a Scandinavian vibe. The lichen adds a wonderfully earthy undertone to the drink. If you don't happen to live in the tundra or taiga, with ready access to lingonberries and reindeer moss, both can be ordered online.

1 quart/1 L vodka
4 ounces/112 g honeycomb
1 plum, pitted and thinly sliced
7 ounces/200 g blueberries
2½ ounces/70 g lingonberries, red currants,
    or cherries (fresh or frozen)
¼ cup/4 g reindeer lichen
1 teaspoon juniper berries
1 sprig each fresh lemon thyme and marjoram

CONTINUED ▶

In a large jar, combine the vodka, honeycomb, and sliced plum and leave to macerate, covered, at room temperature for 2 to 3 days.

After this initial maceration, slightly crush the blueberries and lingonberries and add them to the vodka. Leave to sit for 2 to 3 weeks. Add the reindeer lichen, juniper berries, and herbs and let sit for 1 week more.

Strain the cordial through a fine-mesh sieve, then strain the mixture again through a double layer of cheesecloth. This second straining may require a long, slow drip, so be patient—you want to end up with a refined, clear cordial. Once it is fully strained, transfer the cordial through a funnel into a 1-quart / 1 L bottle and seal well. The cordial will keep, refrigerated, for 3 months or more.

The Pasglas

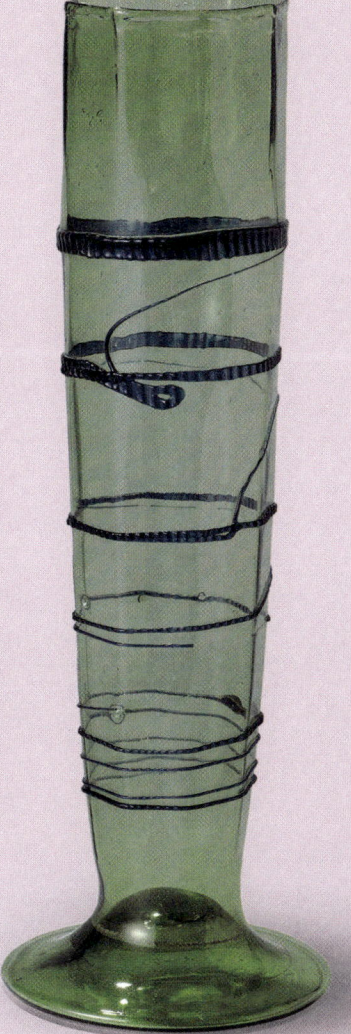

Nineteenth-century Bavarian beer drinkers introduced a fashion for steins—bulbous mugs made of high-quality stoneware frequently ornamented with whimsical figures and humorous slogans. By the twentieth century, beer steins had become objects of cultish desire, with entire museums devoted to the craft. Another vessel designed for beer is much less well known. This is the pasglas, which was used for beer-drinking games in seventeenth-century Holland. Though competing with a pasglas required less physical exertion than, say, modern beer pong, it induced equally rapid inebriation.

A pasglas is tall (nearly 11 inches / 28 cm high), with horizontal glass stringers around the sides that mark measured gradations, diminishing in size from top to bottom. As the glass is passed around the table, each drinker has to gulp the beer down to the next marker. This takes careful calibration: guzzle too much, and you have to drink down to the next stringer; take in too little, and you must do the same. Very few of these glasses have survived, and not only because they were made of poorly blown glass (as you can see from the air bubbles in this example from Amsterdam's Rijksmuseum). As the imbibers got ever more drunk, more and more glasses were broken.

Summer Berry Switchel

Switchel, an early American vinegar drink, is having a comeback, and rightly so, since this fruity, sweet-tart beverage is loaded with nutrients. Switchel's origins are uncertain. We know that the ancient Greeks enjoyed a vinegar drink called oxymel that was sweetened with honey; none other than Hippocrates (of the doctors' oath) recommended it to balance the bodily humors. In colonial America, apple cider vinegar proved a natural base for the drink, with molasses the favored sweetener. Ginger was added for a touch of heat.

We find molasses a bit heavy on the palate, so we temper the drink's acidity with honey and add some lemon juice for brightness. Our recipe also gives a nod to that other colonial vinegar drink, shrub, by including a variety of fresh berries, allowing us to play with the flavor profile. (You can find our recipe for Cranberry-Orange Shrub in Preserved: Fruit.*)*

Switchel was initially enjoyed by American farmers at harvest time—hence its alternate names of "haymaker's punch" and "harvest drink"—making it the eighteenth-century equivalent of Gatorade, thanks to its cooling and restorative powers. If we're to believe the 1964 Old Farmer's Almanac, *the popular beverage soon moved from the fields into the hallowed halls of Congress. There, nineteenth-century senators would avail themselves of the drink from a huge punchbowl positioned in the center of the chamber to allay their thirst during the muggy Washington summers. The congressional switchel, unlike its rural counterpart, was liberally spiked with rum—possibly contributing to the era's overblown oratory.*

---

10 ounces / 280 g summer berries, such as strawberries, raspberries, blackberries, and/or blueberries

4 cups / 1 L water

½ cup / 120 ml raw apple cider vinegar

¼ cup / 84 g honey or more, depending on desired sweetness

2 tablespoons freshly grated peeled ginger

2 tablespoons freshly squeezed lemon juice

A few sprigs of fresh herbs like lemon balm, lemon verbena, thyme, or mint

In a blender, combine the berries with 2 cups / 475 ml of the water and the vinegar, honey, ginger, and lemon juice. Purée until smooth. Pour into a large glass jar or pitcher and add the remaining 2 cups / 475 ml water and the herbs and stir to combine. Refrigerate the mixture overnight. The next day, strain the switchel and taste for sweetness, adding more honey if desired. Transfer to a clean 1-quart / 1 L jar or flip-top bottle. Serve the switchel well chilled. It will keep in the refrigerator for at least 1 month.

Aged Eggnog

A drink composed primarily of dairy products mixed with a combination of spirits and spices is admittedly strange. Its journey may have begun with the hot beverage known as posset, which called for milk to be boiled, then curdled with wine or ale and other ingredients, including eggs, spices, sugar, and breadcrumbs. Posset famously makes an appearance in several of Shakespeare's plays, most notably when Lady Macbeth drugs King Duncan's guards with the drink. Aristocrats enjoyed posset from a decorative two-handled vessel with a spout, known as a posset pot or cup.

In eighteenth-century colonial America, that early drink evolved into a spiced and spiked milk punch—eggnog—which came to be associated with the Christmas season, especially in the American South. Caribbean and Latin American cultures also have variations on the punch. Eggnog's etymology is a bit, shall we say, milky. The presence of eggs is obvious enough, but the suffix could derive from the Old English word "grog," strong beer, or from "noggin," a small wooden cup.

Once a staple of American holiday celebrations, eggnog has become something of a relic, no doubt partly because commercial versions are thickened with cheap additives such as gelatins rather than with real milk, cream, and eggs. Even the addition of rum or bourbon can't correct for inferior ingredients. We believe it's time to resurrect this smooth, boozy milk punch. Entertaining is easy when you prepare the eggnog base in advance. Let it age for a few weeks or up to a year in the refrigerator, where its flavor mellows. When guests arrive, simply measure out the amount of base you want, strain the spices from it, and shake it with fresh milk and cream. This base also makes an elegant dessert recalling a French sabayon.

EGGNOG BASE
MAKES ABOUT 1 QUART / 1 L

12 eggs
1½ cups / 360 ml bourbon
½ cup / 120 ml brandy
¼ cup / 60 ml amontillado sherry
⅓ cup / 80 ml dark rum
1 cup / 240 ml pure maple syrup
½ teaspoon salt
2 cardamom pods, smashed
½ teaspoon black peppercorns
1 (1-inch / 2.5 cm) piece of ginger, peeled and finely grated
1 vanilla bean, split lengthwise
2 cloves
2 allspice berries
1 (½-inch / 1.25 cm) piece of cinnamon stick

In a large bowl, vigorously whisk the eggs, bourbon, brandy, sherry, rum, maple syrup, and salt until well mixed. Place the spices in a 1-quart / 1 L glass jar, pour the egg mixture over them, and seal the jar with a lid. Shake well and transfer to the refrigerator. Age for at least 3 weeks before using. The base will keep for up to 1 year; just remember to shake the jar once a month.

EGGNOG
MAKES 2 SERVINGS

¾ cup / 180 ml strained Eggnog Base
6 tablespoons / 90 ml whole milk
3 tablespoons / 45 ml heavy cream
1 ice cube
Nutmeg, for grating

CONTINUED ▶

In a cocktail shaker, shake the eggnog base with the milk and cream for 30 seconds, until nice and frothy. Add the ice cube and shake for another 15 seconds, until the shaker feels cold. Strain the eggnog into a chilled glass and grate a bit of nutmeg over the top. Serve immediately.

EGGNOG SABAYON
SERVES 2

¾ cup/180 ml strained Eggnog Base
½ cup/120 ml heavy cream, whipped to
    stiff peaks
Grated nutmeg, ground cinnamon, or cocoa
    powder, to garnish

In a medium bowl, beat the eggnog base with a hand-held electric beater until light and pale yellow, approximately 1 minute. Alternatively, you can whisk it by hand, though it will take longer and require more muscle.

Bring a small pot of water to a slow simmer and place the bowl over it, making sure that the bowl doesn't touch the water. With a hand whisk, continue beating until the eggnog is thick enough to coat the back of a spoon, 8 to 12 minutes; the mixture should fall on itself in gentle mounds.

Pour into small dessert glasses and serve with a generous topping of freshly whipped cream and a dash of nutmeg, cinnamon, or cocoa.

Fire Cider

Besides its use as a condiment for prime rib and other meat and fish dishes, the root vegetable known as horseradish is valued for its medicinal properties. Its uses have included treating urinary tract infections, lowering blood pressure, and even fending off gout.

Herbalist and teacher Rosemary Gladstar is credited with combining horseradish with cider vinegar, garlic, ginger, spices, and herbs and letting it rest for a month, then adding honey to the strained liquid to balance the heat. In 1981, she published her work, calling it fire cider, a drink she developed to provide an immunity boost during the damp and chilly Northern California winter. Fire cider has since become a go-to digestive aid made commercially by a few brands as a wellness tonic.

Our version, which includes dried hibiscus flowers and lemon for added flavor, leaves the lips tingling the way a Szechuan meal does, thanks to the capsaicin from the chile peppers. The sensation moves down the tongue to the throat, providing a warming effect. Fire cider also boosts the spirit and bestows a sense of overall well-being.

½ pound / 225 g shallots, peeled and thinly sliced

10 cloves garlic, peeled and minced

2 or 3 hot chiles, such as serrano or jalapeño, thinly sliced

3 ounces / 84 g horseradish, peeled and coarsely grated

3 ounces / 84 g ginger, peeled and coarsely chopped

1 ounce / 28 g turmeric, peeled and coarsely chopped (or 1 tablespoon turmeric powder)

1 ounce / 28 g dried hibiscus flowers

½ teaspoon cayenne

1 whole lemon, quartered and thinly sliced

1 cinnamon stick

2 star anise

1 teaspoon coriander seed

12 black peppercorns

4 cardamom pods, smashed open

6 sprigs lemon thyme

6 sprigs cilantro

Approximately 1 quart / 1 L raw apple cider vinegar

½ cup / 170 g honey (or more, depending on desired sweetness)

Place all the roots, fruits, herbs, and spices in a 2-quart / 2 L glass jar and pour in enough cider vinegar to just barely cover all of the ingredients. Screw on a nonmetallic lid (or a metal lid lined with waxed paper to keep the vinegar away from the metal). Shake the jar well and let it sit in a cool, dark place, shaking every few days to distribute the ingredients. Leave the fire cider to steep for 30 days.

Once the cider is ready, strain out the solids and stir in the honey. Store the cider in small glass bottles or jars in a dark cupboard. It will last more or less indefinitely.

Mango Tepache

Fermented, plant-based drinks contribute a wide range of exciting flavors to Mexican cuisine. Many of these drinks originated in pre-Hispanic times as ritual libations for priests and gods. The most familiar might be pulque, made from the sap of the agave plant. Drinks fermented from corn, such as tepache, tejate, tejuino, and tesgüino, are still popular throughout Mexico today.

Of these ancient beverages, only tepache has gained an audience in the States, no doubt because it is the sweetest and the easiest to make. After the Spaniards colonized Mexico and established new trade routes from South America, pineapple largely replaced corn as the base for tepache, in a no-waste method that calls for fermenting pineapple peels with piloncillo, a raw cane sugar. Pineapple tepache is said to have originated in the western state of Jalisco. In Veracruz, to the east, a wild black cherry called capulín makes a popular base, while in Oaxaca a special springtime tepache is prepared by fermenting the pads of the cardón cactus into a beautiful, fuchsia-colored drink. Oaxaca is also home to tepache de tibicos, made from the granules that grow on the pads of prickly pear cacti.

Here, we use mango to yield a sweet tepache with a lovely caramel flavor from brown sugar. If you don't have piloncillo or muscovado on hand, you can substitute the lighter sucanat, though you'll want to use ¾ cup/109 g of it. No matter the type of sweetener, it never hurts to spike the finished drink, as Mexicans often do, with tequila, mezcal, or beer.

---

4 ounces/112 g piloncillo or jaggery, or
  ½ cup/110 g muscovado sugar
5 cups/1.2 L filtered water
10 ounces/280 g ripe mango, cut into chunks
1 tablespoon tamarind paste
½ teaspoon coriander seed, toasted

If using piloncillo or jaggery, chop it into small pieces. Pour half of the water and all of the sugar into a 2-quart/2 L jar, stirring well to dissolve. Place the remaining water in a blender along with the mango and tamarind paste; purée until smooth. Add the mango purée and the coriander seed to the jar and stir to combine.

Cover the jar with cheesecloth; use a rubber band or jar ring to hold it in place. Leave on the counter at room temperature for 2 to 4 days, stirring daily, until small bubbles appear (the fermentation time will depend on how warm the room is; in cooler conditions, it will take longer). Once the tepache is actively fermenting, strain it through a cheesecloth-lined fine-mesh sieve, squeezing out all of the liquid. Discard the pulp.

Divide the tepache between two 3-cup/750 ml flip-top bottles or other sealable jars and leave for another day or two on the counter to ferment a little more, opening and resealing the bottles daily to release the built-up gas. Once it's fizzy, refrigerate the tepache before serving. It will keep for 3 to 6 months, though its sweetness will dissipate over time.

Lassi

The culinary cultures of hot climates worldwide feature all sorts of drinks that miti-gate the heat. In places where spicy food is the norm, these drinks also soften the burn of chile peppers. Some of the most delicious hot-weather drinks are lassis, which are popular throughout India. The lactic acid from lassi's cultured yogurt base soothes the palate when eating even the spiciest curries.

Lassis originated in Punjab, in India's northwest, a region that fell under Mughal domination from the sixteenth through the eighteenth centuries. The Mughals popu-larized the use of yogurt in cooking, though Ayurvedic medicine had long touted both its cooling effect and what we now know are its beneficial probiotic properties.

Lassis can be made either savory or sweet. Aromatic spices, such as cardamom and ginger for sweet lassis and cumin for savory ones, add welcome dimension to the drinks. Sweet lassis are often enhanced with puréed fruit or nuts, such as mangoes and cashews. Here, we make an especially creamy version by blending the yogurt with coconut milk in place of water.

Prepared lassis will keep, covered, for 3 days in the refrigerator. Whisk them lightly before serving.

YOGURT

MAKES ABOUT 1 QUART / 1 L UNSTRAINED
YOGURT OR 1½ TO 2 CUPS / 360 TO 475 ML
STRAINED YOGURT

1 quart / 1 L whole milk
2 tablespoons self-propagating yogurt starter
    or store-bought full-fat
    plain yogurt

In a large stainless-steel pot, gently warm the milk over low heat to 180°F / 82°C, stirring occasionally so that the milk doesn't scorch. Once it has reached the proper temperature, remove the pot from the heat and leave the milk to cool to 110°F / 43°C (you can accelerate the cooling process by setting the pot in a large bowl filled with ice), stirring it from time to time. Once the milk has cooled sufficiently, whisk in the starter. Transfer the mixture to a yogurt maker and let it culture undisturbed for about 6 hours, until it thickens.

Alternatively, you can pour the mixture into canning jars or other nonreactive containers and cover them loosely with lids. Set the con-tainers in a slow cooker or a dehydrator set at 110°F / 43°C. You can also incubate the yogurt in an oven first heated to 115°F / 46°C and then turned off. Wrap the jars in a couple of layers of towels to keep them warm as they incubate. Oven-cultured yogurt will take a few hours longer than yogurt incubated in other ways.

Once it is made by any of the above methods, the yogurt can be stored in the refrigerator for up to 2 weeks.

To make thicker, Greek-style yogurt for the lassis, place the prepared yogurt (or 1 quart / 1 L of store-bought full-fat plain yogurt) in a cheesecloth-lined strainer set over a deep bowl. Leave the yogurt to drain at room temperature for 8 hours or overnight. The whey can be used to make the Strawberry-Anise Whey Soda (page 94). CONTINUED ▶

SAVORY LASSI

MAKES 2 (8-OUNCE / 236 ML) DRINKS

In some parts of India, savory lassis are briefly smoked over cow dung or charcoal. You can approximate this process indoors by setting a small metal bowl in a larger one. Pour the lassi into the large bowl, then place a hot chunk of charcoal in the small one. Cover the large bowl tightly with aluminum foil and let the smoke infuse the lassi for 3 to 5 minutes, depending on how smoky a taste you desire.

1 cup /240 g strained yogurt
1 cup /240 ml water (or more, depending on
    desired thickness)
¼ teaspoon ground cumin
1 tablespoon chopped fresh mint leaves
¼ teaspoon salt

Place all the ingredients in a blender and whiz briefly until smooth.

COCONUT-ROSE LASSI

MAKES 2 (8-OUNCE / 236 ML) DRINKS

This extra-creamy lassi is our ode to Chennai's beloved Kalathi Rose Milk Shop, which has been in business for nearly a hundred years. Their original rose milk is made with rose syrup; here we substitute more readily available rosewater and add a splash of grenadine to turn the lassi a gorgeous shade of pink.

1 cup /240 g strained yogurt
1 cup /240 ml full-fat coconut milk (or more,
    depending on desired thickness)
2 tablespoons raw honey
1 teaspoon rosewater
2 teaspoons grenadine syrup
¼ teaspoon ground cardamom
⅛ teaspoon salt

Place all the ingredients in a blender and whiz briefly until smooth.

SPICED MANGO LASSI

MAKES 2 (12-OUNCE / 354 ML) DRINKS

Here we make the classic lassi flavor of mango even more enticing by spicing it up with vanilla, cardamom, cinnamon, and ginger.

1 cup /240 g strained yogurt
1 cup /240 ml water (or more, depending on
    desired thickness)
1½ cups /285 g diced mango, fresh or thawed
    from frozen
2 tablespoons raw honey
½ teaspoon vanilla extract
¼ teaspoon ground cardamom
⅛ teaspoon ground cinnamon
¼ teaspoon ground ginger

Place all the ingredients in a blender and whiz briefly until smooth.

HOT CHOCOLATE

The Maya Chocolate Cup

Long before the naturalist Linnaeus classified chocolate as *Theobroma cacao*, "the food of the gods," the indigenous Maya of Central America were preparing a thick, frothy drink to honor their gods in ritual celebrations. They often added achiote paste to the ground cacao beans, turning the mixture vermilion, to recall the sacred blood offered up in sacrifice. *The Popol Vuh*, the K´iche´ Maya book of creation, relates that cacao was one of the ingredients used to create human life, and it remains essential to Mesoamerican cosmology, linking the earthly cycles of life and death to the heavenly one of rebirth. Oaxacan families continue to drink hot chocolate at Day of the Dead celebrations, visiting the graveyard to pour a cup for their ancestors and then returning home to drink chocolate at their own feast table.

To make chocolate, cacao pods are fermented until the interior pulp breaks down and releases the cocoa beans inside. These beans are then sun-dried and ground into a paste. The Maya mixed this paste with hot water, frequently adding seasonings such as hot chiles, cinnamon, allspice, and dried flowers. Though commoners likely drank the chocolate from gourds, the nobility used painted earthenware cups, elaborately decorated with glyphs describing the cups' function. A server would dramatically pour chocolate from a large vessel held at shoulder height into a smaller one below, thereby aerating the drink and creating plenty of froth, considered the drink's most precious part.

Pompelmocello

This beautiful grapefruit liqueur is a variation on limoncello, Italy's bright-yellow lemon liqueur. So beloved is limoncello that various creation myths link it to ancient traditions, but more likely it dates back only a century to the island of Capri, where an innkeeper named Maria Antonia Farace dreamed up the liqueur for her guests. Her great-grandson trademarked the name "Limoncello di Capri" in 1988. Some years later, the fragrant, oval Sorrento lemons used to produce limoncello received a PGI (protected geographical indication) designation from the EU, specifying their precise growing and harvesting conditions.

Like limoncello, pompelmocello contains only vodka, water, sugar, and citrus peel, in this case mainly grapefruit. The long steeping of the peel ensures that all of its essential oils are transferred to the alcohol to convey intense flavor. Be sure to use unwaxed organic grapefruit when making this liqueur, as the rind is where any residual chemical spray lingers. If you can't find ruby reds in full blush, the liqueur will be less pretty but equally tasty. A few sprigs of tarragon are a delicious addition, or you can add another herb of your liking. Serve straight from the refrigerator as a postprandial digestif.

12 large, unwaxed organic ruby red grapefruits, rinsed clean
2 unwaxed organic lemons, rinsed clean
1 (750 ml) bottle 100-proof vodka (about 3 cups)
1½ cups / 300 g granulated sugar
750 ml water (about 3 cups)
3 sprigs fresh tarragon, plus more for bottling (optional)

Using a microplane, zest the grapefruits and lemons, taking care to avoid the bitter white pith; you should end up with 1 to 1½ cups / 54 to 72 g zest. Place the zest in a 2-quart / 2 L glass jar or other nonreactive, sealable vessel and pour the vodka over it. Close the jar tightly and leave the vodka to steep in a dark place for 4 weeks, by which time it should have taken on a lovely pale pink hue.

Unscrew the jar and carefully scoop up some of the zest to see whether all of the essential oils have been extracted from it. If they have, the zest will be white and brittle, and you are ready to proceed. If not, let the vodka steep for another week.

In a medium saucepan over low heat, dissolve the sugar in the water, then set the pan aside and let the syrup cool to room temperature. Once it is cool, pour the syrup into the vodka mixture, adding the tarragon if desired. Stir well and seal the jar again. Set it in a cool, dark place for another 2 weeks.

Place a fine-mesh sieve over a bowl and line it with cheesecloth. Carefully pour in the syrup to strain out the solids. With your hands, gather the ends of the cheesecloth and squeeze out all the remaining liquid so that the zest is as dry as possible. Discard the zest. Taste the liqueur. If you want it sweeter, make a little more simple syrup by boiling together 2 parts water and 1 part granulated sugar until the sugar dissolves. Once the simple syrup has cooled, you can add it to the grapefruit liqueur.

Transfer the liqueur to bottles or jars and cap them tightly. If you like, you can add another sprig of tarragon to each bottle. We like this liqueur best chilled, but it can also be served at room temperature, or straight from the freezer for an extra-refreshing drink. It lasts indefinitely.

Pu-erh Vodka

The practice of infusing vodka with fruit and natural or artificial flavors has led to some of the more dubious products in the modern-day spirits industry. These flavored vodkas vary from "electric raspberry lemonade," an enticement to barely legal bar-goers, to quality vodkas flavored with orange or vanilla and other high-minded attempts to enhance what is essentially a flavorless base spirit. While commercially available vodkas are hit or miss, this recipe, combining the earthy, fermented tea known as Pu-erh with vodka, offers a rich, slightly bitter jolt when sipped neat or on the rocks. It is also a versatile and easy-to-make infusion that will yield delightful results in a cocktail.

Pu-erh derives its name from a city in Yunnan province in southwestern China. The most common form of Pu-erh is tea leaves that have been steamed and compacted into a cake. The moisture trapped in the tea leaves encourages the growth of microorganisms, including fungi, and this fermentation begins to change the tea's chemical composition and, ultimately, its flavor as it ages. While Pu-erh's origins as a tea with medicinal properties date back two thousand years, it is prized today for its depth and mysterious allure. It is one of a few teas that produce a sensation that the Chinese call hui gan, *or a sweetness that lingers in the throat after an initial hit of bitterness. The variety known as sticky-rice Pu-erh is a particular favorite of ours.*

Steeping Pu-erh leaves in vodka transfers this sensation and perhaps even amplifies it, giving the spirit a distinct taste and bewitching aroma. The resulting drink requires no marketing gimmicks or flashy packaging. Here, we offer both the vodka-based infusion and a recipe for Pu-erh simple syrup, along with a cocktail that combines the two with a sea buckthorn base. Befitting its geographical journey across the Asian continent from China to Russia, this cocktail is called the Siberian Express.

---

3 tablespoons / 12 g fermented Pu-erh tea
    leaves
½ cup / 120 ml water
1 cup / 240 ml vodka

Place the tea leaves in a small heatproof cup. In a small saucepan, bring the water almost to a boil, then pour it over the leaves and steep the tea for 10 seconds. Strain off the liquid through a fine-mesh sieve. Discard the liquid and place the tea in a small jar. Add the vodka and allow the mixture to infuse for 2 to 12 hours, depending on how strong you like it. Strain through a fine-mesh sieve into a bottle and refrigerate or freeze until ready to use. The vodka will keep indefinitely.

PU-ERH SIMPLE SYRUP
MAKES ABOUT 1 CUP / 240 ML

3 tablespoons / 12 g fermented Pu-erh tea
    leaves
1 cup / 240 ml water
¾ cup plus 4½ teaspoons / 170 g granulated
    sugar

Place the tea leaves in a small heatproof cup. Bring ½ cup / 120 ml of the water to a boil in a small saucepan. Pour the water over the leaves and steep for 10 seconds. Strain the tea through a fine-mesh sieve. Discard the liquid and set the tea leaves aside. CONTINUED ▸

In a small pot, bring the remaining 1 cup / 240 ml of water to a boil. Turn off the heat and add the tea. Steep for 3 minutes. Add the sugar, stirring to dissolve it. Strain through a fine-mesh sieve. Allow the simple syrup to cool to room temperature, then store it in a small jar in the refrigerator until ready to use.

SIBERIAN EXPRESS COCKTAIL
MAKES 2 COCKTAILS

4 ounces / 120 ml Pu-erh Vodka (page 41)
¾ cup / 180 ml Sea Buckthorn Base (recipe follows)
6 tablespoons / 90 ml Pu-erh Simple Syrup
2 tablespoons freshly squeezed lemon juice
Crushed ice
2 lemon twists (optional)

In a rocks glass, stir together the vodka, sea buckthorn base, simple syrup, and lemon juice. Add a generous handful of crushed ice and serve right away. If you want to brighten the cocktails, top them with a twist of lemon.

SEA BUCKTHORN BASE
MAKES ABOUT 1 PINT / 475 ML

4 cups / 512 g fresh or frozen sea buckthorn berries, or 1½ cups / 360 ml sea buckthorn juice
6 tablespoons / 126 g raw honey

Put the sea buckthorn berries through a food mill. Transfer this purée (or the juice, if using) to a medium bowl and stir in the honey. Pour the mixture into a 1-pint / 500 ml jar and chill in the refrigerator for 1 hour before using. The base keeps for at least 1 month in the refrigerator.

Peaches and Cream

Milk punch was on the endangered species list of cocktails for most of the nineteen hundreds, but it has rightfully rebounded in the twenty-first century as mixologists embrace its versatility and viscosity. No other alcoholic beverage can mimic the texture of milk punch, a drink created when a mixture of alcohol and acid is used to curdle milk, resulting in a clear, velvety liquid that is left after straining the solids ever so slowly and methodically—for hours, or even days. In fact, it is thought that the lengthy process of crafting a batch of milk punch is what led to its near demise, as Americans in the New World lacked the patience of their English forebears.

This punch prolongs the lifespan of ripe peaches by macerating them in a liquor-citrus mixture before adding milk and beginning the long process of straining out curds and other solids. The result is a liquid that is pink-hued and slightly cloudy in comparison to a truly clarified milk punch. It makes for a smooth, creamy, fruity cocktail that stands ready to drink for several weeks.

1 pound / 454 g ripe peaches, pitted
2 tablespoons tightly packed fresh mint leaves
⅓ cup / 57 g raw cane sugar
Zest of 1 lemon
6 tablespoons / 90 ml freshly squeezed
    lemon juice
12 tablespoons / 177 ml freshly squeezed
    lime juice
¼ teaspoon salt
½ cup / 120 ml fino sherry
¼ cup / 60 ml amaretto
1¼ cups / 300 ml white rum
1 cup / 240 ml whole milk

In a blender, purée the peaches, mint, sugar, lemon zest, lemon juice, lime juice, and salt until smooth. Add the sherry, amaretto, and rum and pulse to combine. Transfer the mixture to a 2-quart / 2 L jar. Cover tightly and leave the mixture to macerate at room temperature overnight. The next day, shake the mixture to recombine it, then strain it through a fine-mesh sieve, pressing hard on the solids to extract all the liquid. Discard the solids.

Place the milk in a nonreactive 2-quart / 2 L container or jar. Pour the strained boozy mixture into the milk in a slow but steady stream—don't be tempted to do this the other way around, as the milk won't curdle properly. Stir the mixture once, then cover the container and leave the milk to curdle undisturbed for 1 hour.

Set a sieve over a large bowl and pour about half of the curdled mixture into it. Let the mixture drain until the liquid has flowed out (you can gently scrape the sides of the sieve to encourage the liquid to flow). Discard the solids, then repeat with the remaining curdled milk. Again, a gentle scraping is fine but don't press down hard on the solids. This process is slow—it can take up to an hour—so try to be patient. Once again, discard the solids and rinse out the sieve.

Line the sieve with cheesecloth and place it over a clean bowl. Restrain the mixture. This step will take 30 minutes to an hour, but it's fine to let it drip overnight. The strained punch will be free of solids but still slightly cloudy in appearance due to so much puréed fruit.

Serve the punch over ice in a rocks glass. It will keep in the refrigerator for at least 3 weeks.

Pear and Caraway Kvass

Though vodka may come first to mind as Russia's most iconic beverage, kvass, an effervescent refresher popular long before distilled alcohol came onto the scene, is the true national drink. Classic kvass is naturally fermented from sourdough rye bread and water, with a little honey added to promote fermentation. It can be flavored with spices like coriander and caraway seed and herbs like lemon balm, mint, and tarragon. Lemon juice is often added. Russian monasteries were once famous for the elegant varieties of kvass they produced.

During Soviet times, thirsty pedestrians in need of a quick pick-me-up regularly made a beeline for the bright yellow and red tanker trucks parked on street corners. Everyday kvass was sold on tap for mere kopecks, though the communal glass was not for the faint of heart, as it was only perfunctorily rinsed in between servings.

Kvass can also be made from vegetables and fruits. Beet kvass is traditionally added to borscht, and when drunk straight, it's a rejuvenating tonic. Some of our favorite kvasses are made from fruit. In mid-summer, we favor raspberry kvass, while we reach for pears as the days grow cool. Here, we've heightened the subtle flavor of fresh pears by adding dried ones as well. Dried apples would have a similarly delicious effect.

A word of warning: Kvass is lively. As it ferments on the counter after bottling, be sure to open the bottles a couple of times so the gas doesn't build up. Otherwise, you might be met with a wild eruption when opening a bottle for the first time. (It's always a good idea to place the bottle in the sink and hold an overturned bowl over it to catch any liquid that might shoot into the air.) Kvass should be stored in the refrigerator, where its bubbles will settle down and its flavor will continue to evolve.

1¼ pounds / 560 g very ripe organic pears (4 or 5)

2 cups / 100 g organic dried pears, cut into thin strips

1½ quarts / 1.5 L water

1½ to 2 teaspoons caraway seed, to taste

1 teaspoon aniseed

2 tablespoons mild raw honey

¼ cup / 60 ml freshly squeezed lemon juice

1 heel of unseeded, preservative-free rye bread, very lightly toasted

8 raisins

Cut each unpeeled pear into quarters and remove the stems; you don't have to remove the seeds. In a food processor, pulse the fresh and dried pears into a coarse mash, then transfer it to a large stockpot. Add the water, caraway seed, and aniseed and bring to a rolling boil, then immediately remove the pot from the heat. Allow the liquid to cool until it's lukewarm, about 105°F / 40°C. This will take several hours.

Stir the honey and lemon juice into the warm liquid. Pour this mixture into a 1-gallon / 4 L jar and drop in the heel of bread. Cover the jar with cheesecloth and leave at room temperature for 2 to 4 days, stirring the mixture vigorously two or three times a day. CONTINUED ▶

PEAR AND CARAWAY KVASS CONTINUED

Once you're ready to bottle the kvass, scald two 2-cup/500 ml flip-top bottles with hot water. Strain the pear mixture through a double layer of cheesecloth into a 1-gallon/4 L jar, pressing down hard on the solids, then wringing the cheesecloth to extract the last bit of juice. Discard the pulp.

Using a funnel, pour the kvass into the bottles, adding 4 raisins to each one. Seal and leave the kvass to ferment at room temperature for another 6 to 8 hours, then transfer the bottles to the refrigerator. The kvass will continue to ferment slowly in the refrigerator and will keep for several weeks. Serve well chilled.

The Traveling Tea Ceremony Set

Tea ceremony sets in Japan reflect more than five centuries of tradition, during which the drink has been used variously for meditation, celebration, negotiation, and as an expression of Zen simplicity. The tea ceremony ritual evolved from its origins in Chinese Buddhist monasteries, where tea was originally drunk for medicinal purposes. The Japanese practice known as chadō—the "way of tea"—represents a sort of enlightenment that comes from the making and drinking of matcha, the powdered green tea that is whisked into a frothy drink. Tea ceremonies are performed in a dedicated space and choreographed according to the seasons. The utensils can vary; part of the art lies in the tea master's choice of objects, which are accorded as much respect as the tea itself.

Practicing the tea ceremony with the proper materials is sufficiently important that traveling kits were devised during the seventeenth century. The box is made of lightweight paulownia wood. This set is robustly stocked with some of the distinctive accoutrements of the ceremony, including a lacquered caddy for holding the matcha, a long-handled bamboo ladle for drawing hot water, and ceramic chawan or tea bowls—a taller one for wintertime use to keep the tea hot, and a shallower one, for summertime, whose greater surface area allows the tea to cool quickly. Beneath the chawan are a cotton cloth to wipe the bowls and a ceramic pot to hold clean water. The lowest shelf holds a pot for waste water and a small bamboo rest for the utensils when they're not in use.

Horchata de Morro

The creamy drink known as horchata is based variously on grains, nuts, and seeds. In Valencia, Spain, it's a cinnamony beverage made with chufa—so-called tiger nuts—which are actually not nuts at all but the tubers of yellow nutsedge. In Mexico, horchata is prepared with white rice as a type of agua fresca, a cold, refreshing drink. In Puerto Rico, toasted sesame seeds reign supreme, while Salvadoran horchata is based on morro seeds from the calabash tree, which is more familiar for the decorative gourds carved from its dried fruit.

Although horchata is closely identified with Hispanic and Latino food cultures, it is not native to those parts of the world. The original drink was devised from barley, a grain prized in ancient Egypt, Greece, and Rome for purposes both medicinal and ritual. Barley's Latin name, hordeum, *gave rise to the word* hordeata, *which eventually evolved into* horchata. *When the Moors invaded Spain in the eighth century, they introduced the beverage. Eight centuries later, the Spaniards brought it to Mexico, along with rice and sugarcane, leading to the Mexican style of the drink.*

We've opted to make our horchata in the lively Salvadoran style with morro seeds (which are readily available online), cacao nibs, and plenty of spices. The finished powder can be held for months in the pantry, ready for mixing with milk or water at a moment's notice.

HORCHATA SPICE MIX

MAKES ABOUT 6 CUPS / 575 GRAMS

HORCHATA MIX

2¼ cups / 225 g morro seeds
½ cup / 67 g unhulled brown sesame seeds
½ cup / 66 g raw peanuts, skins removed and halved
½ cup / 60 g pumpkin seeds
½ cup plus 2 tablespoons / 116 g white rice
½ cup / 62 g cacao nibs
3 tablespoons / 15 g coriander seed
2 teaspoons aniseed
2 whole cardamom pods
4 cloves
1 teaspoon kosher salt
1½ tablespoons pure vanilla powder
2 tablespoons ground cinnamon

In a large skillet, lightly toast the morro seeds, then transfer them to a large bowl. Repeat with the sesame seeds, peanuts, and pumpkin seeds, toasting each ingredient separately and adding them to the morro seeds. Set the bowl aside.

In the same skillet, lightly toast the rice until fragrant and golden and transfer it to a clean bowl. Repeat the process with the cacao nibs, coriander seed, and aniseed, again toasting each ingredient separately before adding it to the toasted rice. Stir in the untoasted cardamom pods and cloves, along with the salt, vanilla powder, and cinnamon. Pour this mixture into a blender or spice grinder and purée to a fine powder. Scrape the powder into the bowl with the morro seed mixture, mixing well to combine.

In a food processor, working in small batches, gently pulse the combined mixture until it is finely powdered, scraping the first batch into a clean bowl before processing the next and adding it to the bowl. The nuts and seeds are oily, so be careful not to overgrind the mixture into a paste.

Store the horchata mix in a sealed container at room temperature for up to 3 months.

CONTINUED ▶

HORCHATA DRINK

MAKES 1 DRINK

2 tablespoons horchata spice mix
½ cup / 120 ml milk (cold or warm)
 2 teaspoons maple sugar, brown sugar, or
    honey (or more, depending on desired
    sweetness)

Pour the milk into a blender and add the spice mix and sweetener. Purée on high for 10 seconds, then strain through a cheesecloth-lined sieve. Serve in mugs or glasses.

The Demitasse Cup

Thanks to its stimulating effects and its source, coffee has been called "the wine of Araby." And indeed, in pre-coffee days the Arabic word for coffee, *kahwah*, was used in poetic reference to wine. In Africa and the Middle East, where coffee culture originated, the beverage is consumed in small, strong doses. In the US, it is more often enjoyed from a mug or a large cup. In between lies the European practice of demitasse, which literally means "half a cup." These smaller cups, half the size of standard Western teacups, originated in mid-nineteenth-century France as an elegant way to serve strong coffee after a meal. This practice was picked up by high society elsewhere, as well as by those who aspired to sophistication. For instance, until Vassar College became coed, Vassar girls would retire after dinner for demitasse in their dorms' living rooms, where they drank coffee from small cups with their pinkies crooked in affectation and used miniature silver spoons engraved with the VC monogram.

The gilded demitasse cup and saucer you see here were manufactured around 1900 by the venerable English Coalport Porcelain Factory. The cup stands about 1¾ inches / 4.5 cm high. Demitasse cups come in many styles. Some resemble espresso cups, with straight sides that are sometimes rippled at the top; others, like the one here, have wide bowls like teacups. To emphasize their uniqueness, demitasse cups are always sold separately, not as part of a standard place setting.

Amaro

Amaro *is Italian for "bitter," though the word has become something of a catchall for any bittersweet, herbaceous, Italian-made liqueur. Amari (the plural form of amaro) are typically offered as a digestif—their medicinal mix of spices, herbs, and barks implies that they can settle the stomach after a rich meal. But as amaro has become more widely used in recent years, the once-dusty bottles have moved forward in liquor cabinets and on bar shelves to be employed as an aperitif or as a flavor-packed mixer in sours, spritzes, and citrusy cocktails.*

The complex production of amaro seems best left to Italian families working from centuries-old recipes, although a few noteworthy brands have emerged in the United States. We hope this recipe will encourage you to enter the fray and add your own unique touches—though it will require patience and perseverance! For one thing, sourcing the ingredients seems daunting, given the mix of bitter barks, unheard-of herbs, and dried flowers, in addition to spices, roots, and citrus peels. Then there's the matter of macerating these elements in the base spirit, creating a sugary syrup, mixing the two, and then aging them for months or longer.

Yet don't let this stop you. Creating a DIY amaro will yield the ultimate beverage-making bragging rights, and the obstacles are easy to overcome. Start by searching the internet for "botanicals near me" to find a spice or herb shop where you can source the roots and other ingredients. Our recipe calls for a mix of overproof vodka and brandy for its neutral spirits base, which are easy enough to find at most liquor stores. For aging, we provide three different methods, with oak and without.

1 (750 ml) bottle high-proof or overproof vodka (about 3 cups)

1 (750 ml) bottle brandy (neutral, not too sweet; about 3 cups)

1 teaspoon gentian root

½ teaspoon orris root

1 teaspoon roasted dandelion root

1 teaspoon rhubarb root

1 teaspoon wormwood

1 teaspoon angelica root

1 teaspoon burdock root

3 tablespoons aniseed

1 tablespoon black peppercorns

1½ teaspoon whole cloves

3 tablespoons whole black or green cardamom pods

1 tablespoon mace blades

1 tablespoon coriander seed

1 tablespoon caraway seed

1 tablespoon juniper berries

1 tablespoon dried lavender flowers

1 tablespoon dried rose petals

1 tablespoon dried chamomile flowers

3 tablespoons dried orange blossoms

3 sage leaves

4 fresh or dried bay leaves

1 sprig marjoram or oregano

¼ cup / 6 g tightly packed fresh mint leaves

1¼ cups / 300 ml dry white vermouth

¾ cup / 180 ml distilled water or boiled and cooled water

1½ to 2 cups / 145 to 195 g dark muscovado sugar (depending on desired sweetness)

½ cup / 52 g dried sour cherries

½ cup / 67 g dried Angelino plums or dried apricots (about 6)

¼ cup / 37 g golden raisins

1 lemon, thinly sliced

1 orange, thinly sliced

CONTINUED ▶

Pour the vodka and brandy into a 1-gallon / 4 L jar or crock. Add the gentian root, orris root, dandelion root, rhubarb root, wormwood, angelica root, and burdock root to the jar. Seal the jar with a lid and place it in a cool, dark place for 2 weeks, swirling daily. Strain the liquid through a fine-mesh sieve lined with cheesecloth. Discard the solids and pour the liquid back into the jar.

Place the aniseed, peppercorns, cloves, cardamom, mace, coriander seed, caraway seed, and juniper berries in a mortar and gently pound them to crack the spices open. Add the cracked spices to the strained liquid along with the dried flowers and herbs, close the jar tightly again, and macerate the mixture for 5 days in a cool, dark place. Once you've set this mixture aside, combine the vermouth, water, and sugar in a 2-quart/2 L wide-mouth jar, close it tightly, and store it next to the other jar for the same 5-day period. The sugar will gradually dissolve to create a vermouth simple syrup.

After 5 days, strain the spice-infused alcohol through a fine-mesh sieve into a bowl or other large vessel. Set the sieve with the solids aside for the moment. Rinse the jar or crock of any rogue herbs and return the infused alcohol to it. Cover tightly. Transfer the strained herbs and spices into the jar with the vermouth syrup. Add the dried fruit and fresh citrus, pressing down lightly on the fruit to make sure it's immersed. Let both mixtures steep for another 7 days in a cool, dark place.

After 7 days, strain the infused and sweetened vermouth through a fine-mesh sieve into the large jar with the infused alcohol. Let this mixture sit for 3 days, then filter it through a paper coffee filter.

At this point you have several options. You can transfer the amaro into one or more flip-top bottles, or ones that can be sealed with a cork, and leave it to age in a cool, dark place for 6 to 8 months.

Alternatively, you can make the flavor more complex by aging the amaro on oak. Either pour the amaro into a large jar with a tight-fitting lid and add 2 tablespoons toasted oak chips, or pour it through a funnel into a 3-quart / 3 L toasted oak barrel that has been soaked and prepped according to the manufacturer's specifications.

Stored in a cool, dark place, the amaro will keep more or less indefinitely.

Tejuino

If you love corn as much as we do, you're sure to fall for the earthy taste of tejuino, a refreshing drink from the Mexican state of Jalisco. Tejuino originated in pre-Columbian times among the indigenous people of the Sierra Madre mountain range, who use the drink in their celebrations. It gets its sweet caramel boost from unrefined cane sugar.

Tejuino is prepared with masa—the same fresh corn dough used for tortillas and tamales—which is easy to make at home: You just stir water into the finely ground corn flour known as masa harina. Masa harina differs from regular corn-meal in that it has undergone nixtamalization, which involves cooking and steeping dried corn in calcium hydroxide. This increases the available content of calcium, niacin, and fiber.

You can serve tejuino in showy fashion by pouring it into glasses from on high to produce foam. It becomes even more special when you top the drink with a traditional scoop of lime sorbet, which mimics nieve, the beloved Mexican frozen treat.

TEJUINO BASE
MAKES ABOUT 5 CUPS / 1.2 KG

4½ cups / 1.1 L water
8 ounces / 225 g panela or piloncillo
2 cups / 256 g masa harina
¼ cup / 60 ml freshly squeezed lime juice

In a large pot over high heat, bring 3½ cups / 830 ml of the water to a boil and add the panela or piloncillo. Stir until the sugar is completely dissolved, then remove the pan from the heat.

In a large bowl, mix the masa harina with the remaining 1 cup / 240 ml water until it resembles moist sand. Slowly stream in the boiling water, whisking until the mixture is fully combined.

Return the mixture to the pot and cook over low heat, stirring frequently to make sure that it doesn't scorch, until the mixture thickens enough so that when you run a spoon along the bottom of the pan, the line it makes slowly fills back in. The masa can take anywhere from 5 to 25 minutes to thicken, depending on how finely ground it is, so keep a close eye on it.

Remove the pan from the heat and let the masa cool for 30 minutes, then stir in the lime juice. Transfer to a medium bowl and cover with cheesecloth and a loose lid. Leave the mixture to ferment at cool room temperature (68° to 72°F / 20° to 22°C) for 3 days, until it is fully set. If any mold forms on the top of the mass, gently scrape it off and cover the mixture again. Once fermented, the base will be quite thick and have a mildly sour flavor. Use the tejuino base right away or refrigerate for up to 1 month.

TEJUINO DRINK
MAKES 2 DRINKS

1 cup / 240 g Tejuino Base
1 cup / 240 ml cold water
2 tablespoons freshly squeezed lime juice
Pinch of salt
Chamoy sauce (optional)
Crushed ice
Lime sorbet (optional)

Place the tejuino base, water, lime juice, salt, and a splash of chamoy sauce in a blender. Purée on high until smooth. Serve immediately over crushed ice. For an extra-refreshing treat, top with a scoop of lime sorbet.

The Jícara

Mezcal is revered in Oaxaca. This drink reflects the region's terroir, distilled as it is from any number of different species of agave, each with its own distinctive taste. The flavor of mezcal can range from earthy to grassy to spicy, citrusy, or floral, though all mezcals share a smokiness from their production process. Piñas—the agave hearts—are roasted for several days in an underground pit, then crushed and fermented before the juice is distilled in small stills. Mezcal is usually aged for several months, though it can be aged for years.

Making mezcal demands both time and expertise. Mexicans' respect for the drink is reflected in the jícara, the traditional vessel crafted for serving it. The jícara is named after the jícaro or calabash tree, whose gourd-like fruits are used to make these drinking bowls. After the fruit is cut in half, the pulp is scraped out and the thick skin is boiled and dried. Artisans polish, paint, and engrave the gourds with stylized decorations of the region's animals and plants, as well as geometric patterns. For serving, the jícara is set on a base of plaited reeds or palm fronds so that it won't tip over.

The jícara's wide mouth allows the intense aroma of mezcal to disperse gently upward rather than attacking the nose. And because jícaras are slightly porous, they always absorb a little mezcal, adding complexity to the drink's flavor with each subsequent use.

Qamar al-Din
Over-the-Moon Apricot Nectar

Qamar al-Din, sometimes called amardeen, *is a thick apricot nectar enjoyed through-out the Middle East. It is considered a staple during Ramadan, when it is served just before iftar, the meal that breaks the daily fast. Made from apricot paste dissolved in water, qamar al-din is, like dates, a high-energy food that rapidly restores the blood sugar. It can be made thick enough to eat with a spoon or thin enough to drink.*

The drink's poetic name translates from the Arabic as "the moon of religion," which has led to much speculation about its origins. Most sources claim that it was first drunk centuries ago—by an Egyptian caliph or a handsome Syrian man—during apricot season, which that year coincided with the new moon of the lunar month that ushers in Ramadan. It is further claimed that the drink's origins are Syrian, with its name derived from a variety of apricots grown near Damascus. Until the current civil war, Syria was indeed one of the world's largest exporters of apricot paste. The war displaced many traditional producers, who now make the paste in the rebel-held province of Idlib.

But the story takes a turn as we dig deeper. As early as the fourteenth century, the explorer and travel writer Ibn Battuta described an exceptionally tasty apricot in Konya, Turkey, that likely lent qamar al-din its name. This explanation may have seemed too prosaic for such an exquisite drink, and so a folk etymology arose that poetically links it to the moon.

---

7 ounces / 200 g apricot paste or fruit leather
4 to 5 cups / 1 to 1.2 L water
2 tablespoons orange blossom water
¼ cup / 60 ml freshly squeezed
    lemon juice
2 tablespoons honey
Ice
Toasted and chopped pistachios or pine nuts,
    for serving

Cut the apricot paste or leather into 1-inch / 2.5 cm pieces. Place them in a bowl and add 2½ cups / 590 ml warm water. Cover and leave at room temperature for 2 hours, as the fruit softens into the water; then chill in the refrigerator for 8 hours or overnight.

After it has chilled, scrape the softened mixture into a blender. Add the orange blossom water, lemon juice, and honey and purée until completely smooth. Add another 1½ cups / 360 ml cold water to the blender and whir once more. If the consistency seems too thick, dilute the drink with an additional ½ to 1 cup / 120 to 240 ml cold water. Serve well chilled over ice, garnished with chopped nuts.

Qamar al-din can be held in the refrigerator for at least 3 weeks. For longer keeping, pour it into ice cube trays and freeze for up to 3 months. Just pop out the cubes and thaw as needed. It also makes great popsicles.

Şalgam

Kombucha is the current darling among fermented drinks, but it may be time to consider another—one that packs even more of a health punch and doesn't contain hefty amounts of sugar. That drink is Turkish şalgam, made by fermenting purple carrots, and often turnips, with bulgur. By the time it's ready to drink, şalgam has turned a brilliant magenta, a color we intensify by adding red beets.

Şalgam hails from southern Turkey, where it's a classic accompaniment to the city of Adana's famous ground-lamb kebabs. A glass of rakı—anise liquor—is often consumed as a chaser. Şalgam can be enjoyed as is or spiced up by stirring in hot pepper before serving. The drink is traditionally presented with spears of brined carrots poking up from the glass.

Purple (sometimes called "black") and yellow are the original colors of wild carrots, which were domesticated around present-day Afghanistan; Dutch horticulturalists developed orange carrots only in the seventeenth century. If you can't find the purple variety, feel free to use standard orange ones, though they don't have the same antioxidant and antiradical properties that the anthocyanins in purple carrots provide.

½ pound / 225 g purple or red carrots
½ pound / 225 g purple-top turnips
½ pound / 225 g red beets
2 tablespoons dried chickpeas
¼ cup / 37 g coarse bulgur
2½ tablespoons / 22 g kosher salt
3 cups / 720 ml warm water
2 tablespoons freshly squeezed lemon juice,
    or more to taste

Wash the carrots, turnips, and beets and set them aside. Peel only the beets, then chop all the vegetables into ½-inch / 1.25 cm pieces. (It's worth taking the time to chop them neatly, since they make delicious pickles.)

Place the chickpeas and bulgur in a piece of cheesecloth and tie it with twine to make a parcel. Place the vegetables and the parcel in a 2-quart / 2 L jar.

In another jar or a bowl, dissolve the salt in the water, then pour this brine over the vegetables. Place a piece of parchment paper or plastic wrap directly against the vegetables and weight it with a plastic bag filled with water, a glass fermentation weight, or a clean rock to keep them submerged. Allow the mixture to ferment at room temperature (68° to 72°F / 20° to 22°C) for 3 to 4 weeks. Unscrew and gently re-screw the lid each day for the first week, then once a week after that to release any gas that builds up inside the jar.

After 3 weeks, taste the liquid to determine if it is sufficiently sour—it should have a nice lactic tang. Once the şalgam is ready, discard the chickpea and bulgur parcel.

Stir in the lemon juice and place the jar in the refrigerator. When you're ready to drink the şalgam, strain off as much of the liquid as you want and serve the drink well chilled. It will keep for several months. CONTINUED ▶

ŞALGAM BLOODY MARY BASE

MAKES ABOUT 1 QUART / 1 L, ENOUGH FOR
8 DRINKS

*This Bloody Mary has plenty of zing,
thanks to the addition of pickled vegetables
and horseradish. For truly electrifying
flavor, we recommend using our recipes
for homemade Worcestershire sauce and
the beet-red Eastern European horseradish
called* chrain, *both of which can be found in
the* Condiments *volume of our series.*

8 ounces / 225 g red beets, topped and washed
Olive oil
8 ounces / 225 g drained pickled vegetables
    from the Şalgam (about 2 cups)
2 tablespoons tightly packed fresh parsley leaves
1 garlic clove
½ cup / 120 ml Şalgam liquid
1½ cups / 360 ml vegetable juice, such as V8
1 tablespoon raw honey
3 tablespoons freshly squeezed lemon juice
1 teaspoon Worcestershire sauce
2 tablespoons horseradish or chrain
½ teaspoon freshly ground black pepper
Scant ¼ teaspoon kosher salt
Small ice cubes
Hot sauce or Worcestershire sauce, to taste
Vodka

Preheat the oven to 400°F / 200°C. Place the
beets in a pan with a splash of olive oil. Cover
the pan and bake the beets until a knife easily
pierces them, 1 to 1½ hours. Cool and peel
the beets, then cut them into small pieces.
Place them in a blender along with the drained
pickled vegetables, parsley, garlic clove, and
the şalgam liquid. Purée on high until smooth,
scraping the sides down as needed. Add the
vegetable juice and blend again, then add
the honey, lemon juice, Worcestershire sauce,
horseradish, black pepper, and salt and purée
for a couple of minutes, until smooth.

For each drink, fill a tall cocktail glass with
1 cup / 108 g small ice cubes. Add ½ cup /
120 ml Şalgam Bloody Mary base and
3 ounces / 90 ml vodka. Stir to combine.
Taste for seasoning, adding a little more
Worcestershire sauce and / or hot sauce,
if desired.

ŞALGAM BLOODY MARY

MAKES 1 DRINK

1 cup / 108 g small ice cubes
½ cup / 120 ml Şalgam Bloody Mary Base
3 ounces / 90 ml vodka

Fill a tall cocktail glass with the ice. Add the
Şalgam Bloody Mary Base and vodka. Stir to
combine. Taste for seasoning, adding a little
more Worcestershire sauce and / or hot sauce,
if desired.

Zapekanka
Spiced Vodka

We think of vodka as colorless and odorless, but the spice-infused vodka known as zapekanka is anything but. This vodka is a gorgeous shade of amber, and redolent with spices. It's also homey. Zapekanka was originally prepared in the massive, wood-burning, Russian masonry stove after the stove had been fired for bread baking. Some old recipes call for baking the vodka at a high temperature just after the bread has been pulled from the oven; others recommend infusing it after the oven has cooled to a gentler temperature, a method we prefer.

One eighteenth-century recipe calls for an entire bucket—a whopping 3¼ gallons/ 12 liters—of anise-distilled vodka, to which an eye-popping number of flavorings are added: cinnamon, cloves, cardamom, pepper, ginger, bitter orange peel, star anise, aniseed, coriander, mastic, caraway, saffron, rosemary, wild pepper, mace, mustard, dill seed, styrax (an aromatic resin), cubeb (a type of fragrant pepper), and wheat or rye berries. Our recipe is much simpler, but warm spices still hold sway.

Unlike other infused vodkas, which are meant to pique the appetite, zapekanka is generally offered as a digestif after a meal. Chekhov's short story "The Siren" describes the bliss of drinking zapekanka on a full stomach: "...domestic, homemade zapekanochka is better than any champagne. After the first shot your entire soul is enveloped by the aroma, as if by a mirage, and it seems like you're no longer sitting at home in your armchair, but are off somewhere in Australia, astride the softest ostrich imaginable..." We can't promise that this drink will transport you to distant climes, but we do guarantee that it will bring you delight.

VODKA

1 (750 ml) bottle high-quality vodka
¼ teaspoon black peppercorns
4 large allspice berries
1 (1-inch/2.5 cm) cinnamon stick
1 teaspoon coriander seed
5 or 6 whole cardamom pods
¼ teaspoon aniseed
1 whole nutmeg
1 whole star anise
2 teaspoons dried bitter orange peel
1 (2-inch/5 cm) chunk fresh gingerroot,
   peeled and sliced

RYE DOUGH

1½ cups/160 g rye flour
½ cup/120 ml water

INFUSE THE VODKA: Pour the vodka into a small (1-quart/1 L) earthenware casserole with a lid, such as a bean pot.

Slightly crush the peppercorns, allspice, cinnamon stick, coriander seed, cardamom pods, and aniseed in a mortar—do not grind them. Crack the nutmeg with a mallet to break off about ¼ teaspoon small, coarse shards. Add all these spices to the pot, along with the star anise, bitter orange peel, and fresh ginger. Cover the pot with the lid.

MAKE THE RYE DOUGH: Preheat the oven to 175°F/80°C. Make a stiff, slightly sticky rye dough by mixing together the flour and water in a small bowl. Press the rye dough all around and over the edges of the lid to seal it tightly. The dough seal should be about 1½ inches/ 3.8 cm thick. CONTINUED ▶

73

Place the pot in the preheated oven and immediately turn off the heat, leaving the vodka in the oven to infuse for 8 hours or overnight (the exact timing isn't crucial). Remove the pot from the oven and let the vodka stand at room temperature for another 8 hours.

If any cracks appear in the dough from the temperature change, repair them with a little newly made dough. Then repeat the process, letting the vodka infuse for another 8 hours in a warm oven and again for 8 hours at room temperature.

Line a fine-mesh sieve with cheesecloth and place it over a bowl. Remove the dough seal from the pot and strain the vodka through the sieve, then pour it into a clean, sealable bottle. Let the vodka sit for at least 1 week to allow the flavors to mellow; the flavor will continue to develop the longer it sits. Store the zapekanka tightly closed in a cool, dark place, where it will last up to several years.

Sima

May Day in Finland is a time of picnics and revelry. Known as Vappu, the Finnish name for Saint Walpurga, it is a multipurpose holiday that combines Walpurgis Night (honoring the eighth-century protectress against witchcraft) and International Workers' Day. The celebrations are always accompanied by sima, a sparkling, lightly alcoholic lemonade traditionally served with funnel cake. Lemons were once an expensive import, enjoyed mainly by the affluent, but during Finland's Prohibition (1919 to 1932), sima became a widely popular substitute for stronger forms of alcohol, even if it doesn't provide quite the same kick.

    Most importantly, sima signals the arrival of spring, a big deal for Scandinavians. The tastiest sima is made with the birch sap that runs in the weeks leading up to the holiday, though making it with water tastes nearly as good. The drink's distinctive flavor comes from a sweetener called fariinisokeri, a blend of dark syrup and granulated sugar. Here, we mix light brown and granulated sugars to approximate this taste; for a slightly different flavor profile, you can sweeten the sima with honey. And, if you like your drinks tart, you can always increase the amount of lemon juice to ¾ or even 1 cup (180 to 240 ml). Birch sap, also known as birch water, is readily available online if you don't tap your own trees (see Notes on Ingredients, page 99).

⅓ cup / 50 g light brown sugar
¼ cup / 50 g granulated sugar
1 unwaxed organic lemon
1 quart / 1 L birch sap
Pinch of active dry yeast
2 raisins

Place the light brown and granulated sugars in a large mixing bowl. With a Y-shaped peeler, shave the peel from the lemon, avoiding the bitter white pith. After you have removed the peel, juice the lemon to get ½ cup / 120 ml, adding more if needed.

In a medium saucepan, bring 2 cups / 475 ml of the birch sap to a boil along with the lemon peel. Reduce the heat and simmer, covered, for 10 minutes. Pour the liquid over the sugar, stirring until the sugar dissolves. Stir in the remaining 2 cups / 475 ml birch sap and the lemon juice and leave the mixture to sit until it is lukewarm.

Stir in the yeast and cover the bowl with a kitchen towel. Leave to ferment at warm room temperature overnight, or until tiny bubbles appear on the surface (this could take up to 24 hours, depending on how warm your room is).

Scald two 3 cup / 750-ml flip-top stoppered bottles and drop 1 raisin into each (the natural yeast on the raisins encourages fermentation). With a slotted spoon, remove the lemon peel from the liquid. Pour the sima into each bottle, filling it no more than two-thirds full. Close the top and leave the sima to ferment at room temperature for 2 to 3 days, until it is nice and bubbly, opening the bottles once a day to allow excess gas to escape. Chill the sima well in the refrigerator before serving. It will keep for up to 2 weeks.

The Charka

In olden days, the Russian aristocracy used a number of distinctive drinking vessels. Many of them disappeared in favor of imported goblets and shot glasses when Peter the Great westernized the country in the eighteenth century. However, the charka, used for vodka, survived and remained as a standard unit of measure until Russia officially adopted the metric system in 1917, just before the Russian Revolution.

The charka is a bowl with a wide mouth, a horizontal handle, and a flat or rounded bottom. It typically stands on one or three feet. In the sixteenth century, when vodka was weaker, a charka held 143.5 ml, or nearly 5 ounces. In 1716, Peter the Great decreed that all soldiers be given a ration of two charkas of vodka a day to keep them happy—very happy, as this was the equivalent of five modern shots.

As a drinking vessel, the charka experienced a renaissance during the late-nineteenth-century Slavic Revival, when jewelers like Fabergé crafted this ancient form using precious metals and stones. Early sixteenth-century charkas were large and shallow, but as vodka increased in strength, they grew smaller. By the time of its revival, the charka had been standardized to 124 ml, or just over 4 ounces.

Charkas were elaborately decorated and often sported fanciful figures, such as the sea monsters you see here. This charka was made with the fragile technique of plique-à-jour, which gives the glass enamel a beautiful luster and translucency when held up to the light, a dazzling effect even if you're sober.

Sweet Potato Fly

Guyana, on South America's northeastern coast, gained independence only in 1966, after many centuries of oppressive colonial rule. Its culinary culture reflects a rich mix of indigenous Arawak practices overlaid with European tastes and cooking methods. The flavors also reflect the influence of the enslaved African, Indian, and Chinese laborers transported to Guyana to work the sugar plantations.

Guyana's most iconic dish is pepperpot, a meat-laden stew made spicy with hot peppers. Pepperpot is prepared with bittersweet cassareep, the juice of shredded cassava that is boiled down until thick and molasses-like. This intensely flavored dish calls for refreshing drinks, and Guyana boasts several distinctive ones besides the ever-popular beer and rum. Mauby, similar to a bitter root beer, is made from the bark of the mabi tree and is often flavored with cinnamon and anise. The Guyanese also enjoy swank or limewash, a simple preparation of limes, lemons, or Key limes mixed with water. But Guyana's most unusual drink, and to our minds the most delicious, carries the charming name of sweet potato fly.

Like cassava, the sweet potato is a staple of Guyanese cuisine, and here it is put to use as a starter for a natural citrus-flavored soda to which warm spices add allure. In case you're wondering about the addition of an eggshell, it makes the drink more healthful. Sweet potatoes are high in oxalates, which bind to calcium and inhibit its absorption. The eggshell compensates. As it dissolves in the citrus juice, it releases calcium carbonate, counteracting that depletion. Since sweet potato fly is only lightly carbonated, we like to add some Ginger-Turmeric Bug (page 8) for greater effervescence.

8 ounces / 225 g grated peeled raw sweet potato
1 orange
1 lemon
6 cups / 1.5 L non-chlorinated water
¼ cup / 28 g grated peeled ginger
1¼ cups / 175 g firmly packed light brown sugar
2 whole star anise
4 allspice berries
1 eggshell, cleaned and crushed
½ cup / 120 ml freshly squeezed lemon or
    lime juice
½ cup / 120 ml strained Ginger-Turmeric Bug
    (page 8), optional

In a large bowl, submerge the grated sweet potato in cool water and gently massage it for a minute or two to remove some of the starch. Drain well, repeat the process, and set the drained sweet potato aside.

With a Y-shaped peeler, peel the orange and lemon and then juice them. Place the peels and juice in a 1-gallon/4 L jar or fermentation vessel along with the water, ginger, sugar, spices, and eggshell, stirring well to dissolve the sugar. Add the drained sweet potato. Stir, cover the jar, and allow the mixture to ferment at room temperature, 68° to 72°F /20° to 22°C, stirring daily for 2 to 4 days, or until the mixture actively ferments. At this point, some of the sweet potato will have risen to the surface, and small bubbles will disperse when you stir the liquid.

Strain the fly through a fine-mesh sieve, add the lemon or lime juice and the bug, if using, and pour into two 1-quart/1 L flip-top bottles, leaving 1 to 2 inches /2.5 to 5 cm of head space. Leave the bottles on the counter overnight, then refrigerate before drinking. The fly will keep for 3 weeks in the refrigerator.

The Qero

Chicha is a nutritious South American drink most commonly fermented from corn, though it can also be made from quinoa, potatoes, yuca, peanuts, and wild fruits. In traditional practice, women chewed balls of moist, crushed maize before spitting the mass into a wooden fermentation trough. Enzymes in their saliva initiated the magical transformation of the corn into a lightly alcoholic, beerlike brew. Though most chicha is now made under more hygienic conditions, it is still considered a sacred drink, thanks to the special status it held in Peru's Inca Empire, where it was presented to the Sun God in elaborate rituals. Many people still sprinkle a little chicha onto the ground before drinking, an offering to the earth that brought forth life-giving maize.

Such a revered drink calls for an appropriately symbolic vessel. In Peru, that vessel takes the form of a qero, a flared cup whose rim is wider than its base. Qeros are generally made of wood or ceramic, though the Inca royalty drank their chicha from metal cups crafted of silver and gold. The wooden and ceramic cups were painted all over in vivid polychrome, including red, orange, yellow, and black. Many qeros were fashioned to resemble animals possessing qualities of courage and strength, such as the jaguar on this vessel, which dates to around 1700. Along with the nourishing beverage, the drinker hoped to absorb the positive qualities that the animals represented.

Julmust

The Nordic solution to a harsh climate is to embrace it. In Sweden at Christmastime (Jul), candles and fairy lights flicker everywhere to ward off winter's darkness. The air is filled with the comforting aroma of warm spices like cardamom, ginger, nutmeg, cinnamon, and cloves as gingerbread cookies bake and mulled wine (glögg) simmers on the stove. Restaurants go to extremes with the julbord, Sweden's extravagant Christmas spread, and serve up julöl, a dark, spicy lager. While various styles of glögg and spiced beer are found throughout Scandinavia, the seasonal soft drink known as julmust belongs to Sweden alone.

Julmust tastes like liquid gingerbread—sweet, malty, and lightly carbonated. The proprietary flavor was invented in 1910 as a nonalcoholic alternative to the Christmas season's traditional drinks; it likely derives from the small beers people once drank to avoid contaminated water. The AB Roberts company remains Sweden's only producer of the syrupy extract, which they license to various producers who bottle the finished drink.

The flavor of julmust is so beloved in Sweden that it makes its way into seasonal candies. And even though the precise formula for the Roberts company's extract remains a well-guarded secret, we've managed to create a homemade version that we think tastes every bit as good as the bottled stuff. Think of Dr Pepper, only spicier and less cloyingly sweet.

¾ cup / 116 g whole rye berries
¼ cup / 80 g whole hazelnuts
¾ cup / 70 g cracked, dark-roasted malted barley
2 quarts plus 1 cup / 2.25 L water
2 tablespoons juniper berries
6 green cardamom pods
1½ teaspoons aniseed
½ teaspoon black peppercorns
1 teaspoon coriander seed
3 tablespoons / 25 g raisins
2 tablespoons chopped dried figs
2 tablespoons chopped dried apricots
3 tablespoons / 25 g chopped dried plums
3 ounces / 84 g unpeeled, finely chopped
    gingerroot (about 1 cup)
1 tablespoon dried bitter orange peel
1 whole mace blade
1 large clove
1 whole star anise
¼ vanilla bean, split
2 (2½-inch / 5 cm) cinnamon sticks

1 cup / 130 g lightly packed muscovado sugar
⅓ cup / 110 g barley malt syrup
¼ cup / 60 g freshly squeezed lemon juice
1 cup / 240 ml strained Ginger-Turmeric Bug
    (page 8)
Sparkling water or club soda

Preheat the oven to 400°F / 200°C. Spread the rye berries and hazelnuts in separate places on a large baking sheet or in two small Pyrex vessels. Set the baking sheet in the oven and toast the nuts for about 8 minutes, until fragrant but not too dark. Remove the nuts from the oven but continue toasting the rye berries until they are quite dark, about 20 minutes more, stirring once to ensure even browning. CONTINUED ▶

In a large, heavy-bottom pot, bring 2 quarts / 2 L of the water to a gentle simmer. Stir in the malted barley and the toasted rye and hazelnuts. Cover the pot and simmer for 1 hour, then turn off the heat and let the mixture steep for 30 minutes. Strain the solids through a fine-mesh sieve lined with cheesecloth. Pour 1 additional cup / 236 ml water over the solids to extract the last bit of flavor. You will end up with about 6 cups / 1.5 L of liquid. Rinse the pot and pour the liquid back in. Discard the solids.

In a mortar with a pestle, lightly crush the juniper berries, cardamom pods, aniseed, black peppercorns, and coriander seed. Add them to the grain liquid along with the raisins, figs, apricots, plums, gingerroot, orange peel, mace, cloves, star anise, vanilla bean, and cinnamon sticks. Cover and bring to a boil. Reduce the heat and simmer the mixture, covered, for 30 minutes. Stir in the sugar and malt syrup. Remove the pot from the heat and add the lemon juice.

Cover the pot and let the mixture sit overnight. The next day, strain it into a 2-quart / 2 L jar and stir in the ginger-turmeric bug. Seal the jar and leave the julmust to ferment at room temperature for 3 to 5 days, until small bubbles appear on the surface.

Pour the julmust into two sterilized 3-cup / 750 ml flip-top bottles, seal them, and let the drink ferment at room temperature for 2 to 4 days, opening the bottles once a day to allow gas to escape. Refrigerate the drink and serve it chilled, diluted with sparkling water or club soda to taste (we like a 2:1 ratio). The julmust will keep for about 1 month.

Amazake

Chicken soup, aka Jewish penicillin, has a Japanese rival in the form of amazake, a highly nourishing rice-based beverage sometimes called a "drinkable IV." Amazake is rice on rice: a marriage of steamed rice and rice koji, the mold culture Aspergillus oryzae *commonly cultivated from rice (*Oryza sativa*). The word* amazake *literally means "sweet alcoholic beverage," and the drink is often a byproduct of the Japanese rice wine sake, made from the lees that remain after the alcohol has been poured off. To make sake, steamed rice is inoculated with koji enzymes that convert the starch into sugar. Yeast is then added, and as the mixture ferments, the yeast converts the sugar into alcohol.*

An even more popular type of amazake is made simply by heating together steamed rice and rice koji, skipping the secondary fermentation with yeast. That's the version we offer here. Served warm, it's a favorite wintertime treat at Japanese temple fairs and at New Year's, since (like chicken soup) it is believed to ward off colds and sore throats. Amazake can also be served chilled. Street hawkers once peddled it in summer to relieve heat exhaustion.

When your amazake emerges from the slow heating of rice or another grain with koji, it smells pleasantly yeasty and has a wonderfully sweet taste. The consistency is as thick as porridge, and in fact many people eat it with a spoon; the thick form can also serve as a sugar substitute in baked goods. The addition of water turns amazake into a drink. Our recipe calls for less water than usual, so that the base can be held in the refrigerator for months, ready to dilute at a moment's notice. Amazake aficionados appreciate the floating rice grains that give the drink texture. If you prefer a creamier consistency, feel free to blend the amazake until smooth.

You can experiment with other grains for the amazake base, such as brown rice, pearl barley, oat groats, or buckwheat, using a ratio of 300 g grain to 270 g dried koji (each grain will have a different volume measure). If you use a firmer grain like brown rice or oat groats, soak it for at least 6 hours or overnight before proceeding.

---

2 cups / 270 g rice koji (readily available for purchase online)

1¾ cups / 300 g short-grain white rice

Gently pulse the koji in a blender with ¼ cup / 60 ml lukewarm water (100°F / 38°C). Let it stand for at least 30 minutes to hydrate slightly.

Cook your grain of choice either on the stovetop or in a rice cooker, using the standard water-to-grain ratio for each particular type.

Once the grain is cooked, transfer it to a bowl and let it cool to 135°F / 58°C. Stir the hydrated koji into the grain until well combined. Place the mixture in a 2-quart / 2 L container and cover it with a lid. Hold in a dehydrator or low oven (135°F / 58°C) for 6 to 10 hours, stirring once after 6 hours, until the mixture tastes very sweet and has a rich, dense smell. If it doesn't seem sufficiently sweet, continue holding it at 135°F / 58°C, tasting frequently so that the mixture doesn't begin to turn sour. CONTINUED ▶

AMAZAKE

Alternatively, the rice-koji mixture can be heated in a rice cooker set on warm. Cover it with a clean kitchen towel and then top with the lid; the towel will keep the lid ajar. It is important that the temperature not rise above 140°F/60°C. After 6 hours, open the rice cooker, stir, and taste as above, continuing to warm the mixture, if necessary, until it has turned sufficiently sweet.

Once the amazake is sweet enough, use or refrigerate it immediately. The amazake will keep for 3 months in the refrigerator. For longer storage, divide the amazake base into small portions and freeze for up to 9 months.

WARM AMAZAKE
MAKES 1 DRINK

½ cup/145 g amazake base
½ cup/120 ml boiling water

Place the amazake base and the water in a blender and carefully purée until smooth, making sure to cover the lid and hold it on tightly since the liquid inside is hot. Drink while still warm.

CHILLED STRAWBERRY AMAZAKE
MAKES 1 DRINK

½ cup/145 g amazake base
½ cup/120 ml cold water or milk of choice
4 large strawberries (about 4 ounces/
    112 g each)

Place the amazake base, water, and strawberries in a blender and purée until smooth. Serve chilled.

The Heishi

Although *sake* in Japanese is a catchall term for all types of alcohol, it is most often associated with the clear, fragrant, wine-like beverage made by inoculating steamed rice with koji mold to activate fermentation. Centuries-old traditions around the brewing and drinking of sake align with tenets of the Shinto religion by demonstrating respect for nature and ancestors. The most well-known of these rituals today is the pouring of sake for one's companions, expressing reverence for community and group harmony. Sake cups vary in size, but for communal consumption tiny ones are often preferred, since they lend themselves to the practice of o-shaku, the ritual pouring of the drink, which is repeated many times over the course of an evening. Reciprocal pouring communicates a bond among those sharing the sake, and the drinker always extends the cup toward the person serving the sake to acknowledge the gift.

Sake is poured from narrow-necked flasks called tokkuri, which are usually made from ceramic so that the sake can be gently heated in them. These flasks evolved from the medieval heishi you see here, pairs of bottles used in Shinto shrines to make offerings to the gods. Unlike ceramic tokkuri, heishi are made of lacquered wood. Especially prized are those made in the medieval Negoro style. After frequent use, the heishi's patina reveals a layer of black under the cinnabar red surface, reminding us that preservation and decay are often bedfellows.

Sarsaparilla Soda

This refreshing, natural soda will carry you back to root beer's roots. When English colonists first arrived on American shores in the seventeenth century, they learned from Native Americans how to steep medicinal teas from foraged plants such as sarsaparilla root, sassafras, wintergreen, and birch bark. Eventually they applied their ale-making expertise to these ingredients, adding yeast to ferment them into low-alcohol small beers. Decades later, back in England, a man named Joseph Priestly invented carbonated water, and fizzy, nonalcoholic root beer, specifically sarsaparilla soda, became one of the most popular flavors.

But here's where things get murky. True sarsaparilla comes from a creeping vine in the Smilax family. Many people confuse it with sassafras, a totally unrelated tree (one reason why the word is pronounced "sasparilla"). Originally, genuine sarsaparilla was sold as a patent medicine to cure all ills from gastric distress to psoriasis, but in its soda form it became a trendy nineteenth-century health drink, like kombucha is today. And the history gets even more confusing. The sarsaparilla root is quite bitter, as was this sarsaparilla soda; whereas root beer, made mainly with sassafras root and birch oil, and often with licorice root, had a softer taste. The two sodas—the bitter and the sweet—existed for decades side by side until sarsaparilla's health claims were debunked in the early twentieth century. At that point commercial root beer gained favor, and sarsaparilla soda largely disappeared from the US market. (The irony is that the sassafras oil used in the production of commercial root beer was itself banned by the Food and Drug Administration in 1960 for its carcinogenic properties.) But the confusion doesn't end there. In Asia, New Zealand, and Australia, sarsaparilla soda remains popular, and the major Australian brewery Bundaberg sells both sarsaparilla soda and root beer. However, its website freely admits that "When it comes to the difference between Bundaberg Root Beer and Bundaberg Sarsaparilla there's a simple answer—aside from the label, there isn't one."

9 cups / 2.1 L water

2 tablespoons cut and sifted dried sarsaparilla root

1½ tablespoons cut and sifted dried birch bark

2 tablespoons cut and sifted dried licorice root

½ cinnamon stick

1 star anise

½ teaspoon aniseed

½ teaspoon powdered ginger

3 juniper berries

1 bay leaf

2 strips fresh orange zest

1 whole vanilla bean

6 to 8 fresh mint or wintergreen leaves

1½ tablespoons cut and sifted dried sassafras root bark

½ cup / 63 g sucanat or light brown sugar

¼ cup / 79 g molasses

½ cup / 120 ml strained Ginger-Turmeric Bug (page 8)

1 (½-inch / 1.25 cm) knob gingerroot, thinly sliced

In a heavy-bottom stockpot or Dutch oven, combine the water, sarsaparilla root, birch bark, licorice root, cinnamon stick, star anise, aniseed, powdered ginger, juniper berries, bay leaf, and orange zest. Slice the vanilla bean lengthwise and scrape the seeds into the pot, then drop in the bean. CONTINUED ▶

SARSAPARILLA SODA CONTINUED

Simmer the mixture gently, with the lid slightly ajar, for 30 minutes. Add the mint and sassafras and simmer for another 10 minutes with the lid ajar. Turn off the heat and stir in the sugar and molasses. Let the mixture steep, covered, for 3 hours at room temperature.

Strain the liquid into a 2-quart/2 L jar, discarding the solids. Add the ginger bug and the slices of fresh ginger. Cover the jar's mouth with cheesecloth, using either the outer ring of the jar or a rubber band to secure it. Leave the liquid to ferment at room temperature for 2 to 3 days, stirring it vigorously once a day, until small bubbles form.

Once it is ready, strain the liquid and funnel it into two 1-quart/1 L flip-top bottles for secondary fermentation, leaving 1 to 2 inches/2.5 to 5 cm of head space to allow room for the carbon dioxide to build up. Leave the bottles on the counter for 5 to 7 days, opening them daily to release the pressure. The fermentation can be quite active, so open the bottles carefully; it's best to do so over the sink or a bowl in case the liquid overflows. Once the soda is fizzy, store it in the refrigerator and use it as a soft drink or add vanilla ice cream to make a sarsaparilla float. It will keep for at least 2 weeks.

Strawberry-Anise Whey Soda

What if you could solve a vexing food-waste issue while creating a delicious, refreshing soft drink? That's the promise of whey soda, which easily transforms a byproduct of yogurt production into a beverage that offers health benefits while quenching your thirst.

The current popularity of thick, creamy Greek yogurt has created a glut of sour or acid whey, a thin, runny liquid that gets strained off to create the yogurt's desirable texture and flavor. On a commercial level, this process creates a seemingly insurmountable amount of waste that threatens to become a pollutant; efforts to find viable uses for the whey include turning it into animal feed or crop fertilizer. By contrast, chefs and inventive home cooks have drawn inspiration from centuries-old techniques, using whey's natural carbonation capacity to create transformative beverages.

Whey retains the favorable microbes, proteins, and bacteria that make yogurt a wellness staple. At the same time, it serves as an activated ingredient for a flavored drink akin to kombucha, but without the need for a SCOBY (fermentation starter). Myriad flavors can be combined with the slightly acidic liquid to create a refreshing beverage; here we use fresh strawberries and raw honey for tang and sweetness, and fennel and anise for a licorice-like undercurrent. The resulting savory-sweet probiotic soda tastes great and has a fizziness that makes it fun to drink.

Whey soda may not solve the world's excess sour-whey problem, but it's half of a kitchen twofer that turns regular yogurt into Greek yogurt and makes the base for a natural soda that keeps in the refrigerator for 2 weeks or more.

1 quart / 1 L sour whey from straining 2 quarts / 2 L plain, full-fat yogurt

1 pound / 454 g (approximately 2 medium) fennel bulbs

2 tablespoons aniseed

1 pound / 454 g strawberries, hulled and quartered

½ cup / 170 g raw honey

5 ½ tablespoons / 85 ml freshly squeezed lemon juice

3 tablespoons / 45 ml freshly squeezed lime juice

To make the whey, place the yogurt in a cheesecloth-lined strainer set over a deep bowl. Leave the yogurt to drain at room temperature for 8 hours or overnight. Save the drained yogurt (now the consistency of Greek yogurt) for another use.

Trim and thinly slice the fennel bulbs. Place 2 cups / 273 ml of the whey in a blender with the fennel, aniseed, strawberries, honey, lemon juice, and lime juice and purée. While the blender is running, stream in the remaining 2 cups / 273 ml whey and continue puréeing until the mixture is smooth. (If your blender isn't large enough to accommodate all of the ingredients, blend them in two batches.) Transfer to a 2-quart / 2 L jar, cover tightly, and leave to infuse overnight at room temperature. Don't worry if the mixture separates.

The next day, strain the solids through a fine-mesh sieve. Using a funnel, pour the strained liquid into two 1-quart / 1 L flip-top bottles and leave them to sit at room temperature for 2 to 3 days, until the soda is active and bubbly, opening and closing them once a day to release any built-up gas. The soda will keep for at least 2 weeks in the refrigerator.

NOTES ON INGREDIENTS

This volume features numerous recipes with ingredients that are likely not in your larder. They can usually be found in your local health food store or Asian or Latino market. Many are also available in the ethnic food or organic sections of supermarkets. In a pinch, all can be ordered online.

BARKS, ROOTS, SEEDS, PODS, BLADES
Certain drinks call for barks or roots to add depth of flavor, or for cardamom pods or mace blades (the dried covering of nutmeg) to impart distinctive notes. A good source for these ingredients is the Mountain Rose Herbs website.

BARLEY MALT SYRUP Syrup made from malted barley grains is a natural sweetener used in brewing; we use it in Julmust (page 83).

BIRCH SAP Birch sap, also known as birch water, is tapped directly from birch trees; we call for it in our recipe for Finnish Sima (page 77). A good brand is Patz Birch Sap Water.

CACAO NIBS Dried cacao beans are cracked and crushed to produce cacao nibs. In this book, we toast them and use them in horchata (see page 53) to impart a nuttier, more bitter flavor than dark chocolate—which, unlike cacao nibs, is made with added ingredients such as sugar and milk.

DRIED ANGELINO PLUMS Bright and tart, these plums have a beautiful red-violet color and high levels of antioxidants. They are plump and dense, and even after drying they retain their sweet-and-sour taste. In our recipe for Amaro (page 57) regular dried plums or dried apricots can be substituted for a slightly different taste: Look for a variety that is slightly acidic.

FLOWERS Recipes in this volume call for dried or fresh flowers including lilac, lavender, chamomile, hibiscus, orange blossoms, and rose petals. Dried flowers can be ordered online from Mountain Rose Herbs and Starwest Botanicals. Fresh are available online at Pacific Botanicals.

HONEY Raw, unpasteurized honey is aways our first choice, since it retains the healthful properties that are lost when honey is heated. In one recipe, Summer Fruit and Lichen Cordial (page 17), we use even more natural honeycomb, which is especially good for infusing.

KOJI Koji is made by inoculating starch with spores from the mold *Aspergillus oryzae* and leaving the starch to ferment. Online primers explain how to make homemade koji from rice or barley, a process that takes about 48 hours. Or you can simply buy fresh or dried koji in Japanese and other Asian markets, or online. The packaging may note that it's the ingredient needed to make Amazake (page 87), which we feature in this volume.

MALTED BARLEY Cracked, dark-roasted malted barley is often used in beer-making to add rich flavor and color. We call for it—and for barley malt syrup—in our recipe for Swedish Julmust (see page 83).

MASA HARINA Also known as nixtamalized maize or corn flour, this Mexican ingredient found in many supermarkets and in Latino markets is a key component of the corn-based drink Tejuino (page 60). Excellent masa harina is sold online at Masienda.

MORRO SEEDS A tree variously known as morro or jícaro produces round, hard fruits with seeds that are ground and used in the making of Salvadoran-style horchata (see page 53). Morro seeds are commonly available in Latino markets or online.

PU-ERH TEA This dark tea from Yunnan, China, adds an earthy, nutty flavor to drinks. It is available as loose leaves or packed into cakes, raw or fermented. In this volume, we recommend using fermented Pu-erh in cake form (see page 41); a version known as nuo mi xiang cha, or sticky-rice Pu-erh, works especially well, adding an aroma and flavor redolent of sticky rice. A good online source is Blue Willow Tea.

REINDEER LICHEN This lichen or moss is native to the Arctic regions, but you don't need to travel to the North to procure it. You can buy reindeer lichen online, but make sure that it is the edible form, not the processed moss that's used for decorative purposes. One good source is Forbes Wild Foods. In addition to being infused into drinks like our Summer Fruit and Lichen Cordial (page 17), reindeer lichen is brewed into a medicinal tea used to treat ailments such as coughs or gastric distress.

SEA BUCKTHORN This deciduous shrub, native to parts of Asia and northern Europe, yields berries that are revered for their healthful qualities. Especially high in antioxidants, sea buckthorn berries and their juice have myriad uses, including in drink recipes like our Siberian Express Cocktail (page 42). The berries are available online from Northwest Wild Foods and Regalis Foods.

SUGARS Some recipes call for sucanat, which is unrefined cane sugar. Brown or white granulated sugar can be used in its place, though they will taste sweeter, so you might want to reduce the amount. Other recipes in this book call for unrefined brown sugars including muscovado (a very dark cane sugar with a lovely toffee flavor), panela or piloncillo, jaggery, and maple, all of which are sweeter than granulated sugar and have greater depth of flavor. We occasionally also use superfine (caster) sugar for quick dissolving.

UMEBOSHI The salty, sour Japanese pickled plums known as umeboshi are an intense umami booster with a bracing hit of acidity. You can make umeboshi with ripe ume plums using a salt pickle and red shiso leaves—or simply purchase the prepared plums at a Japanese market or online.

NOTES ON EQUIPMENT

BLENDERS Countertop blenders get put to use in many of the recipes in this book. In some cases, a food processor can be substituted, though blenders can be more effective for puréeing and pulsing certain ingredients.

CANNING JARS Many preservation recipes require a 1 pint/500-ml glass canning jar with a metal lid for fermentation and storage. For long storage, plastic jar lids or lids lined with parchment paper are a great option, as metal rings can begin to corrode if left in the refrigerator for long periods of time.

CHEESECLOTH Used for straining—and for keeping bugs out of your jars while allowing oxygen in during fermentation—cheesecloth is essential to have on hand for preservation recipes.

FLIP-TOP BOTTLES Several recipes call for flip-top, long-necked bottles; these allow carbon dioxide to expand and provide natural carbonation. The flip tops enable you to release gases as they build and then easily reseal the bottle. These bottles can be purchased online or at specialty or big-box home stores. Look for 1-quart/1 L and 1½-quart/1.4 L bottles.

FOOD MILL An underrated kitchen tool, a food mill—unlike a blender or food processor—allows you to purée while straining out seeds and skins.

FOOD PROCESSOR For recipes that call for shredding, pulsing, and grinding, it pays to have a good food processor within reach, especially one with multiple blade options. It can also be used in place of a blender when necessary, although the texture won't ever be quite as fine.

FUNNELS Transferring liquids between jars can be challenging unless you have a proper funnel. We recommend purchasing a set of different sizes.

HEAVY-BOTTOM, NONREACTIVE PANS Some preservation recipes call for a long, slow simmer. A sturdy, nonreactive pan such as one made from heavy stainless steel won't react with high-acid foods and will keep vegetables and fruits from scorching.

FINE-MESH SIEVE A well-made fine-mesh sieve (or strainer) is essential for straining, especially when a recipe calls for pressing on solids to extract liquid. Some of our recipes call for double-straining, which is straining first through a fine-mesh sieve, then rinsing the sieve and lining it with cheesecloth to capture any last sediment during a second straining.

KITCHEN SCALE Like baking recipes, preservation recipes work best when recipe amounts are strictly followed. Weighing ingredients on a kitchen scale ensures consistency and accuracy.

ROCKS GLASS Several of the cocktails featured here, including the Siberian Express Cocktail (page 42) and Peaches and Cream Punch (page 47), call for a rocks or lowball glass (as distinguished from a tall, slender highball glass).

SPICE GRINDER Fermenting and pickling often require grinding whole seeds and spices, so this affordable countertop device is a great time-saver for many of our recipes. Grinding by hand in a mortar and pestle is more old-school, but completely acceptable.

Y-SHAPED PEELER The ergonomic design of a Y-shaped peeler makes it the best tool for peeling fruits and vegetables. A swivel or straight peeler can be used in a pinch, though these types of peelers make the job more awkward.

INDEX

ACKNOWLEDGMENTS

DARRA GOLDSTEIN

Thanks first to Cortney and Richard, my friends and coauthors. We enjoyed a dream team for this series, helmed by our visionary editor, Jenny Wapner, with whom it's always a joy to work. I'm also thrilled to be working again with another dear friend, designer Frances Baca, who has brought the books to such vivid life. It was great fun working with photographer David Malosh, whose gorgeous photos grace these books, and prop stylist Paige Hicks. Thanks, too, to my agent, Angela Miller, and to Carolyn Insley for guiding the books through production. And finally, I'm grateful for the unfailing support of my sister, Ardath Weaver, and that of my husband, Dean Crawford—for his math genius, his editing, and his endless enthusiasm for new tastes.

CORTNEY BURNS

In gratitude for the time-honored preservation traditions that inspire and enliven our creativity. Thanks to my family for putting up with the plethora of jars and experiments that line our kitchen, and for tasting new and different flavors with wonderment and surprise. To my amazing collaboration team, Darra & Richard; what fun it is to create with you both. I am forever grateful to my literary agent Katherine Cowles, and to all the microbes that make this possible; we humbly thank you!

RICHARD MARTIN

I would like to thank my wife, Sonja, and children Apolline and Loic, for taste testing and allowing my preservation experiments to take over the kitchen for long stretches of time. Thanks also to my extended family: Jan and John, Lee and Lisa, Greg and Patty, and Maddi and Max. Over the years, as a website and magazine editor, I've worked with many inspiring chefs, writers, and friends who expanded my culinary world—thanks to all of you. And to Darra and Cortney, thank you for developing these incredible recipes and allowing us to share them with the world.

Hardie Grant North America
2912 Telegraph Ave
Berkeley, CA 94705
hardiegrantusa.com

Vessels page 12 and 62 from Darra Goldstein's personal
collection.

Photo page 21 by Anonymous, *Pasglas*, 1600–1699.
Rijksmuseum, Amsterdam

Photo page 35 Maya, Late Classic, *Chocolate Cup*, 600–800 CE;
courtesy of Princeton University Art Museum

Photo page 51 courtesy of Joanne Rathe Strohmeyer; from the
collection of Merry White

Photo page 56 courtesy of Cooper-Hewitt, Smithsonian Design
Museum

Photo page 78 courtesy of The India Early Minshall collection,
The Cleveland Museum of Art

Photo page 82 courtesy of National Museum of the American
Indian, Smithsonian Institution (Catalog Number 10/5860);
photo by NMAI Photo Services

Photo page 89 courtesy of The Metropolitan Museum of Art

Published in the United States by Hardie Grant North America,
an imprint of Hardie Grant Publishing Pty Ltd.

Library of Congress Cataloging-in-Publication Data is available
upon request

ISBN: 9781958417133
ISBN: 9781958417140 (eBook)

Printed in China
Design by Frances Baca
Prop styling by Paige Hicks

MIX
Paper | Supporting
responsible forestry
FSC® C020056
FSC
www.fsc.org

FIRST EDITION

Hardie Grant

NORTH AMERICA

ABOUT THE AUTHORS

DARRA GOLDSTEIN the founding editor of *Gastronomica*, is the author of six award-winning cookbooks, including *Beyond the North Wind: Russia in Recipes and Lore,* named one of 2020's best cookbooks by *Forbes.com, Esquire*, and the *Washington Post*. In 2020 she was honored with the Lifetime Achievement Award from the International Association of Culinary Professionals.

CORTNEY BURNS (with chef Nick Balla) built a larder-based kitchen at San Francisco's Bar Tartine; their cookbook *Bar Tartine* won awards from both the James Beard Foundation and IACP. *Bon Appétit* has dubbed her the "godmother of fermentation" for her modern take on ancient techniques.

RICHARD MARTIN is a media executive, lifestyle editor, and writer who started magazines and websites that have grown into major media companies, including *Complex, Modern Luxury* (Manhattan and Miami), and *Food Republic*.